Invest Your Way

Invest Your Way

HOW TO
GROW YOUR WEALTH
ON YOUR TERMS

MARK LAMONICA
SHANI JAYAMANNE

WILEY

First published 2026 by John Wiley & Sons Australia, Ltd

© Morningstar Australasia Pty Ltd 2026

The right of Mark LaMonica and Shani Jayamanne to be identified as the authors of *Invest Your Way* has been asserted in accordance with law.

ISBN: 978-1-394-35223-4

A catalogue record for this book is available from the National Library of Australia

Registered Office
John Wiley & Sons Australia, Ltd. Level 4, 600 Bourke Street, Melbourne, VIC 3000, Australia

For details of our global editorial offices, customer services, and more information about Wiley products visit us at www.wiley.com.

Wiley also publishes its books in a variety of electronic formats and by print-on-demand. Some content that appears in standard print versions of this book may not be available in other formats.

Cover design by Wiley

Set in 11.5/16pts and Warnock Pro by Straive, Chennai, India.

Contents

About the authors

Mark LaMonica is the Director of Personal Finance at Morningstar Australia and co-host of the *Investing Compass* podcast. He oversees Morningstar.com.au, one of the country's top spots for investing insights. Mark has an MBA in Finance and is a Chartered Financial Analyst. His focus is on helping everyday investors make smarter decisions with their money. He's a regular commentator in major Australian media, including the *Australian Financial Review*, *Equity Mates* and *Rask*, and is a regular presenter at investor events. Mark is a trusted voice in personal finance.

Shani Jayamanne is a Director, Investment Specialist, at Morningstar Australia and co-host of the *Investing Compass* podcast. She's a familiar name in personal finance coverage across Australian media. She has appeared regularly in traditional outlets such as the *Australian Financial Review*, the *Sydney Morning Herald* and the *Australian*, as well as before investor groups such as the Australian Shareholders Association and the ASX. She is known for breaking down complicated financial topics in a way that makes sense to everyday investors. Shani has worked in financial advice and at an asset manager. With a focus on promoting financial literacy and independence among minority groups, she is passionate about making financial advice more inclusive.

Prologue

This is a different kind of book about money. We want it to be a trusted resource for investors who have graduated from Investing 101. *Invest Your Way* is for investors who know what a share and an ETF are but are struggling to put it all together to get on the pathway to financial independence.

It isn't a series of definitions of investment products. It isn't a set of tricks to save money or a formula to follow to get rich. It doesn't endorse a specific type of investment product. Rather, it is a conversation about financial independence between two friends and colleagues who happen to be experienced personal finance experts.

We have different backgrounds. We come from different generations. While we share a belief in a set of underlying principles, we've followed different approaches based on our unique circumstances and outlooks. This isn't a book that tells you what to do. It's a book that teaches you how to think — and how to draw on your experiences, goals and circumstances to develop your own unique philosophy to achieve the life you want.

Too much financial commentary focuses on investments rather than on the *people* investing. We believe investors are hungry for a new perspective. The investors we talk to tell us they are tired of aspirational messages that lack the practical steps to put a plan into action. They don't want bewildering and unrelatable jargon and complexity. They want the focus to be on the only thing that truly matters — creating a better life for themselves and their loved ones.

We believe that successful investing depends in large part on self-reflection, on understanding yourself and what you want from life. We spend a fair amount of the book talking about ourselves. Not because we think everyone, or anyone, should follow our approaches. Investing is deeply personal. Far too many investing commentators ignore this. Our personal experiences illustrate the process every successful investor needs to go through, which is thinking about the best approach to meet a unique goal. It's not a call to copy our approach; it's a call to reject the notion that conventional wisdom should be followed blindly.

Warren Buffett famously said investing is 'simple, but not easy'. The part that's not easy is the personal part. It's overcoming our emotional conditioning as humans and a lifetime of ingrained views about how the world works and what is needed to achieve success. Successful investing involves looking inward because you can't separate investing from the investor.

We've designed this book to meet you wherever you are on your journey to financial independence. We want to remind you of things you may have lost sight of in the relentless churn of daily life. We want to teach you new things. We want to inspire you to become more introspective, to get to know yourself a little better. More than anything we want you to gain confidence that you are on the right path. This book is one part theory and one part practical exercises to help you create a plan to achieve financial independence. This is your blueprint to take the next step with your finances and to get everything you want out of life.

Meet Shani and Mark

So who are we? On paper we couldn't be more different. Shani is a 32-year-old millennial. Mark reluctantly admits he is in his mid-forties, because once you hit 46 it's hard to argue otherwise.

Shani migrated from Sri Lanka with her family to Sydney's western suburbs when she was a child. Her family made sacrifices to give Shani opportunities, and she stretched herself to take advantage of them.

Investing wasn't a topic of conversation when she was growing up, and it wasn't until she was an adult that she started to think of investing as a means of transforming her life. She learned this early in her career by observing clients of the prestigious fund manager where she worked. As she gained confidence and knowledge she decided she didn't want to be the only beneficiary of the insights she was accumulating. She wanted to help the people who didn't know the pathway she was on even existed. People who didn't think investing was for them. Shani made her first investment at 23.

His father's banking career meant Mark moved around a lot as a child, from Taiwan, Hong Kong and San Francisco to Sydney's eastern suburbs. He spent his high-school years in a suburb of New York. From an early age, he saw investing as just something people did. He was gifted his first shares when he was ten and bought his first shares as a young teenager. He thought it was natural that people understood how to invest and were comfortable doing it. This worldview was challenged in early adulthood after his parents divorced and his highly educated and accomplished mother was consumed by fear and confusion about what to do with her money and whom to trust.

The start of our conversation about investing

Most people play it safe on their first day at a new job. On Shani's first day, she overheard a conversation about franking credits. Finding she didn't agree with the opinion expressed, she crossed the room to say so to the speaker. That speaker was Mark. Our conversation about investing started that day, and it hasn't stopped since.

Along the way we learned that we shared much more than a cursory view of our different backgrounds would suggest. Above all, we both came to Morningstar to work with individual investors because we wanted our careers to mean more than simply collecting a regular pay cheque.

We view investing as a mechanism to provide our community with the financial security and independence we all seek. Far too many people don't know where to start. Others don't have a clear picture of what success looks like or how to achieve better results. Our jobs, and this book, are our way of helping people start and progress on their journey to financial freedom.

To ignore the influence of each person's unique views on how they approach their finances is a pathway to failure. Our experiences shape the philosophy we bring to dealing with money and the way we invest. Acknowledging how our backgrounds and circumstances impact the way we approach money is not a weakness — it's a strength. And it fundamentally changes the outcomes we achieve.

Far too many conversations about investing rely on conventional wisdom and rules that few people take the time to understand. This isn't surprising, because we are told that what matters is what investment products we buy and sell. Most of us don't notice that more often than not, the people advising us are the ones selling us those products.

We believe in several fundamental principles of investing that don't tell you what to do but act as ballast when you are trying to navigate the challenging day-to-day management of your finances. They are the foundation for our own personal approaches to our own finances and investing, and they help to form a philosophical underpinning for our own particular plans and strategies.

Many of us are familiar with the work of Warren Buffett. Fewer of us know his investment partner Charlie Munger. Buffett has said of Munger that when it came to managing money, no-one better had come along for many, many decades. Perhaps Charlie Munger best summed up the importance of an underlying philosophy to guide actions when he said, 'You can't really know anything if you just remember isolated facts and bang 'em back. If the facts don't hang together on a latticework of theory, you don't have them in a usable form.' This book is the latticework on which we hang our investing approaches.

We occupy a unique position in the financial services industry. We work for an investment research house where the emphasis is on coming up with opinions on shares, ETFs and funds. Yet our roles involve engaging with individual investors. Listening to the Morningstar community, it is obvious that their main struggle is how to go about the *process* of investing. This is very different from what we hear from most market commentators, who focus almost exclusively on investments or what is held in portfolios.

Sitting, as we do, at the nexus of the financial services industry and investors trying to reach their goals, it is clear to us that the approach most people take just doesn't work. We've developed an approach based on the only thing that really matters — using investing as a mechanism to achieve the life you want, which is why this book is your essential guide to achieving financial independence.

Investing your way

Star Wars director George Lucas once observed that we are all living in a cage with the door wide open. A conjurer of space fantasy seems like an odd person to draw on at the start of a book on investing, yet this quote perfectly encapsulates how many people handle their finances. The series of financial decisions the average person makes doesn't stray far from a deliberate plan to create financial dependence.

Charlie Munger was a proponent of *inversion*, a mental model that helps break down the barriers to success in any endeavour. The goal of inversion is to think about a problem backwards as well as forwards. By also considering how to make something worse, you can break down some of the ingrained biases that are holding you back from identifying a solution.

For example, if you were trying to make housing more affordable in Australia, you might usefully consider all the ways to make housing *less* affordable. Approaching the problem in this way could uncover new solutions. Munger's inversion model is the inspiration for the quip: 'All I want to know is where I'm going to die, so I'll never go there.'

We are going to use inversion in this book to highlight areas where the conventional approaches people take with their finances hurts the outcomes they achieve. Interestingly, the actions that would be undertaken to lower returns intentionally mirror the behaviour of many investors. Inversion makes it obvious how counterproductive many pieces of conventional wisdom are to investment results.

How to foster financial dependence

This book is a guide to help you achieve financial freedom, and a good place to try out Munger's inversion method is to outline all the ways that you might create a life of financial dependence.

A life of financial dependence is a life spent on the precipice of financial calamity, a life without choices and options. It is a form of servitude in which your efforts serve the financial interests of others — be that a bank, an employer or anyone else we are beholden to. It means constantly being stressed about money.

You can't become financially dependent on your own. It truly does take a village to foster financial dependence. It starts with education or, in this case, the lack of any formal system of financial education. People lacking basic financially literacy are primed to self-apply the shackles of financial bondage.

First, the actions that lead to financial dependence need to be normalised. How do you normalise financial dependence? Step one: people need to make decisions under the illusion they are doing the right thing. Enter the self-interested cheerleaders of the 'conventional' pathway. Cheers from the bank that profits from larger loans and growing house prices. Cheers from the trading platform that encourages you to trade your way to prosperity while making money from each transaction.

The stage is set to take any cash flows you receive from your employer and immediately convert them into long-term debt.

To encourage high levels of long-term debt, a system is needed that focuses on borrowing capacity determined by the self-interested lender, instead of an independent assessment of what is affordable.

Finally, we need fuel for the fire. A societal focus that celebrates looking rich over building wealth fuels more spending. No-one can see what is in your portfolio, but everyone can see the clothes you wear, the car you drive and the house you live in. Since everything can be financed, anyone can look rich without amassing any wealth. All the ingredients are in place for you to get sucked into the debt vortex. Each increase in income means a larger borrowing capacity, which means more stuff to make you look more successful to people you don't know. Before long, most income goes to servicing debt, with little left for discretionary spending and savings.

There is a certain beauty to this system. In previous generations most of those who found themselves in stressful financial situations were at the bottom of the economic pyramid. Now, many on high salaries find themselves barely getting by.

Does this look like your life? Do you want to prevent yourself from falling into this trap of financial dependence? Read on.

How to use this book to achieve financial freedom

Each chapter in this book follows a similar pattern. There is a discussion of theory to provide context. Our personal stories provide examples of how we have incorporated these lessons into our own lives. And there's an exercise that will help you to see where you stand.

Some of these exercises involve self-reflection. Some involve some maths and are more detailed and time-consuming. Each of them will help you incrementally build a personalised financial philosophy, lay out your goals and create your own investment strategy to achieve those goals. Each chapter builds on what we've covered previously and ends with takeaways that outline how you will use the knowledge gained in the chapter and the exercise in subsequent chapters. By the end, you will have your own plan to achieve financial freedom.

The pathway to financial freedom

Chapter 1

We wrote this book because we both believe that investing has the power to transform lives. We may start out and end up in different places, but no matter our age, income and savings, we can all begin our journey towards financial security and independence. This book provides a blueprint for success, however you define it.

'Whatever we do,' wrote American novelist James Salter, 'even whatever we do not do, prevents us from doing its opposite. Acts demolish their alternatives, that is the paradox.' Part of the allure of youth is the notion of limitless possibilities. The nostalgia for that time stems from the belief that once we could have become anything. This may not reflect how we felt at the time or the actual opportunities we had, so much as how our perception of our lives changes as time passes. The decisions we make as we age tend to reduce our future options. If you pursue one career, it closes off other professional opportunities. Choosing a partner means forsaking potential others. Acts demolish their alternatives.

Just as the process of ageing involves closing off options, investing can open them up. This book is designed to help you on your journey towards financial freedom. Each of us may define such

1

freedom differently, yet one commonality is the notion that freedom is synonymous with choice.

Having an emergency fund means not going into debt when life's inevitable reverses occur. Debt is one important way that financial decisions limit choices. Saving and investing for retirement provide more opportunities to do what you want after you finish work. Investing allows you to retire early, pursue part-time work or switch careers. Investing isn't about getting rich; it's about incrementally improving your future by making choices today with that future in mind.

Gaining financial freedom is more than providing the things you want in life. It also gives you the freedom to escape situations you don't want to be in — to leave an unhealthy relationship or walk away from a toxic work environment.

According to the Australian Psychological Society, the number-one source of stress for Australians is money. Relationships Australia finds one of the leading causes of divorce is financial pressure. Investing is a means to an end, and that end can be whatever you want it to be. But ultimately it is about enabling a better life.

Can everyone transform their lives through investing?

We know that many people reading this book are already investors. Those readers don't need convincing, so for them this chapter is simply a reminder of all that can be accomplished.

We also know that our readers will include investing sceptics. We hear the reasons for this scepticism all the time: investing is too complicated; it's rigged in favour of professionals and the wealthy; it's too risky; it's not for them. Even for people who are already investors, this scepticism can creep into their decision making.

While we wholeheartedly disagree with this scepticism and believe investing is for everyone, we are also sympathetic to these arguments. It's not some baseless conspiracy theory. Given the way investing is presented, these feelings make a good deal of sense.

Shani says...

I grew up in a household where investing wasn't discussed. When I looked at investors, I didn't see anyone I could relate to, anyone who looked like me. It isn't surprising I didn't think investing was for me. One of my first jobs was working in client services at a prominent fund manager. I answered questions about client portfolios and was constantly reviewing account histories. I started to notice the habits that led to success. I saw that making small investments consistently over a long period was the pathway to building wealth. And it occurred to me that there was nothing stopping me from doing the same thing and achieving the same outcomes.

A simple diagram (figure 1.1) shows you at one end of a continuum and your goals at the other. Everything in the middle we've called the *investment industrial complex*, with a nod to Eisenhower's famous warning about the military industrial complex.

Figure 1.1: The investment industrial complex

The investment industrial complex includes all the people and companies that create investment products, give you advice on which investments to buy, help you access those investments and help you deal with aspects of investing such as taxes. Here we're talking about fund managers, brokers, financial advisers, financial analysts, accountants and lawyers.

We have spent our careers in the investment industrial complex. While there are bad actors in any industry, we don't think any of the professions in this industry are fundamentally evil. They are simply trying to make a living by charging fees to investors for their services. We will spend time stressing the importance of minimising these fees, because they all detract from your ability to achieve your goals. For now we want to focus on their motivations.

They all take a cut of the money you save and invest. It isn't surprising that people think investing is for the wealthy. Many of the fees are basis-point fees, which means they take a percentage of how much you invest, so it's natural that they would rather serve wealthy investors than those with less money. Some fees are based on trading activity, which means the more you trade the more money they make, so it's natural they want customers who trade more often.

Like any set of businesses, the investment industrial complex needs to justify the cut it takes. In this case, the justification matters more because the cuts are often large. University of Chicago professor Harold Pollack, who famously wrote that everything you need to know about money fits on an index card, estimated that financial advice fees globally are more than a staggering US$1 trillion a year.

The actions of this group contribute to why people think investing is too complex. To get people to hire them and to justify high fees, the investment industrial complex portrays investing as complex and requiring constant activity and a substantial time commitment.

If you fall for that, you are more likely to hire someone else to do it for you. Like many industries, investing is riddled with jargon that serves to separate insiders from outsiders, reinforcing the notion that to invest successfully you need professional assistance.

Throughout history, successful investors have been portrayed in certain ways. When Mark was growing up, it was perhaps best captured in Oliver Stone's movie *Wall Street*, which gives the impression that a successful investor is a god-like man (yes, they were all men) constantly taking audacious actions by yelling into six phones at once.

The fictional masters of the universe in the movie aren't too different from the way a star fund manager is portrayed in the marketing material — this omniscient genius who works all day and into the night to make all the right moves to beat the market.

The focus on the star fund manager was still around when Shani was growing up, but technology now plays a greater role. Data mining, statistical analysis and having three monitors filled with pulsing charts are sold to the public as the secret to investing success.

In both cases the underlying message is the same: you can't do this on your own. Successful investing is hard. Successful investing requires constant activity, and you don't have the time to do it well. Successful investing requires resources and skills you don't have. Once this message has been pounded into your head you discover that — conveniently — there are geniuses who know everything whom you can hire to help. People with access to fancy technology and complex data. People who know what the efficient frontier is and why your portfolio needs to be perched on it.

We think all of this marketing spin is just that — spin. People will hire someone to help, and we support that. Many readers bought this book to help them on their journey, and we certainly support that! But we believe that with some effort anyone can do this on their own, while paying fees only when absolutely necessary.

You don't need a fancy degree. You don't need to dedicate all your time to managing your investments. And you don't need a lot of money to get started. All you need to do is build some knowledge, come up with a plan designed around your personal circumstances, and apply patience and consistency. Those are the ingredients for using investing to create a better life. That is what we teach you in this book.

Mark says...

Investing has always given me this sense of empowerment. I was in total control of my outcomes. And how many things in life can you truly say that about? It didn't matter what natural talents I was born with or where I went to university. My marks didn't matter or what job I managed to get. And as a natural introvert, it just appealed to me. Investing was this private endeavour in which my efforts and results weren't visible to the outside world. It was all on me. It was up to me to build knowledge. It was up to me to have the discipline to stick to my plan.

Why should you invest?

This is a simple question to answer. There's no practical way to achieve financial freedom without investing. You simply can't save your way to financial freedom. Making more money won't get you there. If you don't save and invest some of it, you will be forever dependent on others.

To illustrate this, we'll explore the *rule of 72*. It's a simple concept. Divide 72 by the annual return to calculate how many years it takes to double your investment. If you achieve a 7.2 per cent annual return an investment will double in 10 years. Too easy. But like everything in investing, some additional nuance helps.

Exercise: How many doubles to financial freedom?

Before getting into the rule of 72, here's a simple exercise for you to try. This is especially critical if you are sceptical about investing. Take a back-of-the-envelope guess at how many times you need to double your money to fund a comfortable retirement.

This will vary based on your age and it will be easier if you have a retirement goal. If you don't have a goal yet, we have you covered later in the book. What did you come up with? Keep this number in mind as you learn about how investing can help you achieve your goals.

Why not investing isn't an option

Every year the investment manager Vanguard releases a chart of 30-year returns for different asset classes. An asset class is simply a high-level categorisation of different types of investments. For instance, shares are one asset class and bonds are another. Using the rule of 72, table 1.1 (overleaf) shows how many years an investment in each asset class would take to double, based on the 2024 edition of Vanguard's chart.

This is a critical chart for anyone on the fence about investing. To have any chance of financial freedom, you need to shorten the time it takes to double your money, and the only way to do that is by investing.

Table 1.1: nominal asset class returns and duration to double
your investment

Asset class	Nominal annual return over 30 years (%)	Years to double investment
US shares	11.10	6.48
Australian shares	9.10	7.91
International shares	8.20	8.78
Australian listed property	7.80	9.23
Australian bonds	5.60	12.85
Cash	4.20	17.14

Source: Adapted from the Vanguard 2024 Index Chart

If you are already an investor, this chart is still important. The
investment industrial complex spends a lot of time talking about
which individual shares, funds and exchange traded funds (ETFs)
to buy. However, the asset classes you invest in matters far more
than picking individual securities for your portfolio. A mix of
asset classes in any portfolio will have the biggest impact on the
outcome. More on this later.

According to a 2023 study at the University of Queensland, the
average Australian works for a salary for 45 years. Assuming
returns over the past 30 years are sustained in the future, an
investor in US shares could double a portfolio 6.17 times during
their working years. An investor who remained in cash would
double their portfolio 2.33 times.

That is a huge difference. Imagine you start with $10 000 and earn
the historic return on US shares. With no additional savings,
you would retire with $673 848 after 40 years. If you earned the
historic return on cash, you would have accrued just $51 848.
The 'safety' of more conservative investments such as cash does
not translate into safety when considering life outcomes. As we
noted at the beginning of this section, there is no practical way to
achieve financial freedom without investing.

Don't forget inflation

Since COVID, periods of high inflation have been felt more acutely than in the recent past. Yet even low levels of inflation can eat away at the spending power of your savings over time. Our first exploration of the rule of 72 did not include inflation. Almost all of the returns you see publicised by the investment industrial complex do not take inflation into account either. They are selling returns and don't want to highlight anything that detracts from that. In theoretical investment land, inflation doesn't matter. In real life it does, because the reason all of us save and invest is to grow our money so we can spend it later. The purchasing power of our assets matters.

Table 1.1 showed nominal or non-inflation-adjusted returns. The picture is different if we use real, inflation-adjusted returns. These returns represent how much purchasing power will increase for each asset class. We will talk about inflation a lot in this book. Financial freedom requires saving and investing money so you can spend it in the future, so it matters how much it is going to cost to buy what you want. Compare table 1.2 with table 1.1.

Table 1.2: real asset class returns and duration to double your investment

Asset class	Real annual return over 30 years (%)	Years to double investment
US shares	8.40	8.57
Australian shares	6.40	11.25
International shares	5.50	13.09
Australian listed property	5.10	14.11
Australian bonds	2.90	24.82
Cash	1.50	48

Source: Adapted from the Vanguard 2024 Index Chart

Inflation changes outcomes drastically and further reinforces the need to focus on the importance of investing to achieve your goals. When we adjust returns for inflation it becomes clear how critical it is to invest in growth assets like shares over the long term. Real returns for US shares are 24 per cent lower than the nominal return. Real returns for cash are 64 per cent lower than the nominal returns.

This is mathematically obvious since allowing for inflation takes away more of a lower nominal return than of a higher nominal return. Many investors struggle with conceptualising this arithmetic, which is why arguments against investing can seem sensible. Once you understand the maths, however, those arguments stop making sense.

It is important to point out that over the 30-year period Vanguard surveyed, inflation was low at only 2.70 per cent a year. Since COVID it has been much higher. In any type of inflationary environment, investing in growth assets like shares leads to much better outcomes.

How inflation impacts retirement savings

The impact of inflation is particularly pronounced over the long term. Saving for retirement is one of the longest, if not the longest, time horizon on a goal you will ever have. As an example, we can consider a 30-year-old with $100000 saved for retirement. In our hypothetical example we can assume our retirement saver will leave the workforce at 65 after contributing $15000 to their super each year and achieving an annual return of 8 per cent with annual inflation of 2.5 per cent. At 65 the account balance would be $4063286.

Sounds impressive. However, that fails to take account of inflation. Remember that what matters is not how much money you have but how much you can buy with that money. The purchasing power of that $4 063 286 portfolio is only $1 712 151 in today's dollars. Not so impressive.

Building wealth is the process of amassing financial assets or passive income to create independence. When we use the rule of 72 to explore how many years it takes to double the real spending power of a portfolio, it becomes painfully obvious that it is impossible to build wealth with defensive assets.

It would take more than their working life for most Australians to double real or inflation-adjusted wealth in cash. With Australian bonds an investor can't even reach two 'doubles' of wealth in a working lifetime.

Did your outcome change?

Has your estimate for the number of doubles needed for your money changed since you learned about the rule of 72? Do you still not know what you should aim for? Later we will outline the steps needed to estimate how much you need for a goal like retirement.

For now, we can use a generic example to come up with an estimate for the number of doubles of savings are needed over a career in order to retire comfortably. The rule of thumb is to have 25 times your spending needs saved for retirement.

Assuming you save 12 per cent of your pre-tax salary a year for 40 years and your salary keeps up with inflation, you will need roughly 5.2 doubles over your working life. Chances are you will need more. Many people don't work for 40 years without interruption. Many find their salary growth falling behind inflation. The larger point remains that investing in defensive assets like cash or bonds will not get you anywhere close to 5.2 doubles.

To reiterate our earlier point, defensive assets feel safe over the short term. They provide security. It feels like the right trade-off to make for people who fear the roller-coaster ride of the sharemarket. The logic behind this view is based on how the trade-off is framed. And this matters. A better way to frame the trade-off is whether you want the perception of security or actual security.

The rule of 72 is a good rule of thumb by which to frame these trade-offs. Saving money matters. But ultimately you will need to invest in growth assets if you are to achieve financial independence. Keep focused on the long term and the doubles you need to achieve your goals. Ignore the periods when the sharemarket doesn't do well and things feel scary. Keep your outlook broad.

Why Mark invests

Right before writing this book I returned from leave that included a stop in Bangkok at my favourite hotel in the world. And I found myself floating in the hotel's beautiful pool doing what I always seem to do there: thinking about investing. Investing, not investments. There is a difference.

I wasn't thinking about a share or an ETF. I was thinking about the process of sacrificing today for a better future. That's investing. It is simply delayed gratification. Skipping a dinner out here and there to go on an amazing trip in 10 years' time. That's only possible if you earn a return that meaningfully exceeds inflation.

Many people either treat investing as a chore or fear it so much they avoid it. They see investing as separate from day-to-day life. But investing is tied to life. Our portfolios represent our hopes and dreams for the future, whether it be security, the trip of a lifetime or a better life for those we love.

Being a successful investor is not about finding the best ETF. It is about integrating your investment strategy and approach with your life in a symbiotic relationship. It is in this context that the necessity of investing for living a better life becomes clear.

My love for this particular hotel in Bangkok can be partially chalked up to nostalgia. I have been staying there throughout my life, and some of the nostalgia comes from my own happy memories. But some of it comes from a time before I was born and what unfolded afterwards.

When my parents first moved to Bangkok in the early seventies, early in their marriage and at the beginning of my father's career, they had little experience outside of the United States. I can imagine how they must have felt. Everything lay ahead of them. Like any newly married couple they must have seen the future as full of promise, with no roadblocks in sight.

This view of a future path free of impediments results in many people failing to achieve their investment dreams. There is no substitute for time and no way to get it back as it slowly slips away — an adage that applies to investing just as much as it does to life.

Floating in the pool and rotating slightly to the left I turned my gaze from where my parents lived to the restaurant where I spent Christmas with my family when I was 21, and I recalled the heated argument with my father over my plan to move to New York after my university graduation. I insisted there was nowhere else worth living. He countered that the world offered too many options to make such a blanket statement. But I knew better, and my decision was final.

(continued)

As it happened, four months after that conversation I started dating my now wife Haley and followed her to Boston. I am writing this book in Sydney, and I've now lived in Australia for more than 10 years. I have never lived in New York as an adult.

Putting yourself in a strong financial position not only provides protection if things go wrong but enables you to take advantage of opportunities that arise. And, as my father tried to tell me all those years ago, life presents an array of opportunities, many of which most of us won't be able to pursue.

My mother recently moved into a retirement community. She has had a storied life since those heady days in Bangkok along the Chao Priya River.

My parents' marriage deteriorated into acrimony and eventually divorce. The life they imagined at the start of their Thai adventure unfolded in ways they couldn't have foreseen.

The residents wandering the halls of my mother's new home have far more memories than possibilities for the future. I would argue those memories are less likely to be of things they owned than of experiences with friends and family. Perhaps they lament the opportunities they failed to take.

They will have achieved various levels of career and financial success. Did they think of their net worth as a marker of success? At a certain point, financial assets provide diminishing levels of security. They become little more than a scoreboard in a game no-one can win.

That hotel in Bangkok opened in 1876. The hallways are lined with pictures of famous guests who passed through on their life journeys. Perhaps I was the first guest to contemplate investing while staying there, but I'm certain I wouldn't have been the first person to think about what I wanted from life and how to achieve it.

Why Shani invests

Throughout history, women have found a way to take back some semblance of financial security in the face of often vigorous societal opposition. Far too many women still face these challenges. The main reason I invest is simple: I know it is the only way I can gain independence and financial freedom.

Financial independence is not a goal that is restricted to one gender. But I want to start with what has made this goal particularly important to me.

I moved to Australia from Sri Lanka as a child. Gold played a similar role for women in Sri Lanka as in other parts of the subcontinent. I was given gold at birth, and gold jewellery at auspicious or significant dates in my life. When I got engaged in 2019 my mother gave me ancestral gold bangles.

The tradition of giving gold stretches back centuries. Bestowing gold is the equivalent of providing women with an emergency fund. If you're in a situation that you need to get out of, you have your gold jewellery. It is easily transported and hidden and can always be exchanged for money.

As we were writing this book, Mark sent me a *New York Times* article about Sri Lanka's new female prime minister. They interviewed a Sri Lankan woman about her hopes for her country's future. She earns $100 a month as a garment worker and describes the challenges of the rising cost of living. Half her salary is spent on baby formula for her daughter. 'We don't need the government providing us with food — we can somehow manage. What we need is a country where I have the space to make a little extra cash so I can invest in my daughter — maybe a pair of gold earrings for her first birthday.'

Mark can be forgiven for asking how gold earrings could possibly be an investment. It doesn't fit the traditional idea

(continued)

of an investment in Western culture. However, for this mother it would be an investment in her daughter's financial independence, ensuring she had something to barter in emergencies, or could avoid being controlled financially.

For many Aussie investors, financial independence has come to mean something quite different. The popularity of movements like FIRE (Financial Independence, Retire Early) has turned the term financial independence into a blanket statement which means you are not, and will not be, reliant on anyone or anything for financial support.

For many of us this may not be a realistic outcome prior to retirement. Yet financial independence is similar to the pursuit of 'success'. Shaped by our experiences and our circumstances, it is deeply personal to us.

Financial independence is an evolving concept. The achievement of each milestone sets another in front of us. Just as we continue to grow as people over our lives we can continue to grow financially.

In my case, I had relatively modest goals. After university, I wanted to cover rent and all my associated living costs. That was within reach for me, and it gave me a sense of personal and financial freedom. Increasing my own financial independence was and remains at the core of my financial goals.

Since then I have married and have achieved growth in my career. My evolving notion of financial independence now means being able to support myself independently regardless of any unforeseen circumstances. I have my own bank account and control of my pay cheques, and I have structured my finances in a way that means I can spend (or save) money in whatever manner suits me. This assures me that I can maintain my independence however my life and circumstances change.

None of us knows what the future will bring. I can foresee no circumstances in which I won't be happy in my relationship. Some people think that keeping funds separate to better navigate a relationship breakdown is crass. I see it as a safety net in case the worst happens. It gives me peace of mind now and it would provide relief if a difficult time were to eventuate.

I feel lucky to have had the opportunity to make these choices. Many are finding alternative ways to build a sense of financial security in the face of the constraints they have. The Sri Lankan mother we spoke about earlier wants to build a secure future for her daughter, within the constraints she faces.

It wasn't so long ago that Australian women faced obstacles to achieving financial independence. It wasn't until 1971 that Australian women were granted loans without a male guarantor.

On my own journey to financial independence my next step is to limit my reliance on my employer.

A common dream is to be able to retire early, to leave a job and not look back. I haven't reached that point yet. I have built my emergency fund to cover four months of expenses. I expect I would be able to find new employment within that timeframe.

I know my understanding of financial independence will continue to evolve. At some point I expect I will no longer rely on a pay cheque to cover my expenses.

Key takeaways

You can't save your way to financial freedom. Getting there will require you to invest in growth assets such as shares. Understanding this concept is foundational to success, as there will be times when it will be hard to keep going. Investing is very different from its portrayal by those who have a vested interest in promoting how hard it is. Your goal is not to replicate investing as it is portrayed but to figure out your own approach designed specifically to help you achieve your unique goals.

The biggest takeaway from this first chapter is the discovery that *you can do this*. Everyone can be a successful investor. This book is designed to iteratively describe the structure needed to build financial independence. As you continue to read, you will define and develop a unique financial goal to help you live the life you want. For now, going through the exercise of estimating how many times you need to double your money will reinforce the reality that investing is not optional for financial freedom. Keep this double estimate handy for when you are tempted to quit investing as volatility starts to scare you.

Develop
a financial
philosophy

We begin with an exercise designed to help you develop your money philosophy. Again, this is not where most investing books start. We know a lot of readers are champing at the bit to hear what they should be invested in. For those readers, a gentle reminder that investing is about patience — think of this as practice.

Developing a philosophy is the process of understanding fundamental truths about yourself and the world; it governs how you interact with the world. A money philosophy is the underlying set of beliefs and values that drive your interactions with money. Whether or not you are aware of it, you already have a money philosophy that influences your actions. It may not be a healthy one, but it exists.

We start to develop a money philosophy in childhood. Think back to the role that money played in your household. You may well have internalised many of these initial experiences. If money was a source of stress and anxiety, you may have absorbed that. If it was plentiful, you may have developed a more carefree view of money. Conversely, money may have been used as a mechanism of control and coercion. In other words, cultural and familial components may underlie your attitude to money, and these views are likely to persist whether or not you are financially secure.

An overarching money narrative that reaches back to your childhood and upbringing is likely to be influencing your behaviour. You may conform to this narrative or you may rebel against it. It may or may not have been actually articulated. At a simple level, this could mean you are by default a saver or a spender, but it could also influence how much you worry about money regardless of your financial situation.

Over time your money philosophy will continue to be refined, influenced by your relationships with others and by your experiences with money.

Nothing we say in this book can alter the influence the past has over your worldview, but we can encourage you to reflect on those experiences and to become more aware of the influence they have. We hope this book will help you build your confidence so you can change the way you view money and better control your financial future.

Define your money philosophy

In developing a money philosophy, your goal is to be more deliberative about your approach to money so that your actions align with your values and what you want out of life. Creating a positive narrative about how your finances should support your life can help you achieve your goals. That is because values-based goals are more stable and personal.

American psychologist Leon Festinger, who coined the term *cognitive dissonance*, observed that we suffer mentally when our behaviour doesn't align with our values. His research showed that if we attach a narrative to a set of consistent habits we are more likely to stick to those habits. Over time deviating from them leads to stress. Maintaining good habits that align with what we want to accomplish helps us achieve our goals.

Later we will go through the process of setting goals and aligning an investment strategy to achieve them. This is the habit formation we want to establish. For now, think how your narrative might wrap around those good money habits. What does financial freedom mean to you? How can you use the increased flexibility it provides to make your life meaningful in a way that aligns with your values? It could be more time with family, a greater focus on taking part in meaningful activities, achieving security or helping your loved ones. Figure out your overarching why.

Exercise: Define your financial philosophy

Consider the following questions and write down your answers to each one in a notebook. Make this an iterative process. Write down what first comes to mind in response to each question. Take some time away before revisiting each answer. Writing things down clarifies your thinking, promotes accountability and provides a basis for reference. We will ask you to do this as you read the chapters that follow. This will become your personalised map to financial freedom.

Gail Matthews, a psychology professor at Dominican University in California, has studied the power of writing down aspirations and goals and found it increases the likelihood of achieving them by 42 per cent. That's a good enough reason for us.

(continued)

Questions and actions:

1. What was the prevailing attitude to money in your household when you were growing up? Think specifically about the emotions associated with it.

2. How do your formative experiences with money impact your philosophy now? Are you copying patterns from childhood or resisting them?

3. What do you believe financial freedom would enable in your life? We'll get to specific goals later but for now try to think about your values and how money enables or obstructs them. A value is an underlying belief that drives behaviours and the intention here is to become aware of the values that promote positive behaviours. We tend towards an aversion to connecting money to our underlying values but try to resist that. For example, spending more time with your loved ones could be enabled by financial freedom if it allowed you to cut back on time spent at work or to shorten your commute – or to travel together.

4. Rank your values. Life is about trade-offs and trying to 'have it all' often leads to achieving nothing. Just because something is ranked lower on your list doesn't mean you can never achieve it. Financial freedom is a journey, and most people achieve freedom by degrees across time.

5. Categorise the things you spend most on. You don't need a detailed dollar by dollar budget here – instead look at big categories like housing, cars/transport, food, school fees, entertainment/travel and so on. Include savings here. Estimate the percentage you are spending on each of these high-level categories.

6. Line up your values against the percentage you spend in each category.

The point of this exercise is to give you insights into where you are spending your money and to compare that with what is most important to you. This may be eye-opening and help you to realign your spending. Or perhaps it will simply reinforce what you already know — for example, that housing is expensive in Australia. The point is to reinforce that life is about trade-offs and each of us should strive to go for the ones that will help us to achieve the financial freedom we seek.

Weave the answers to these questions together into a positive narrative around your finances by focusing on the desired destination of your journey. We each craft narratives around different aspects of our lives. In some we are the hero and in some we are the victim. Your money philosophy is your opportunity to craft a positive narrative about your financial life and to define how your finances will enable you to achieve the life you want.

Mark's money philosophy

When I'm interviewed about my money philosophy I often tell a story from my early twenties. The background is that I spent my adolescence in Greenwich, Connecticut, an affluent suburb of New York City. Characterised by all the trappings of wealth — big houses, fancy cars and expensive private schools — Greenwich was the picture of society's conventional view of success.

In my mid-twenties I was staying at my parents' house and commuting to New York. Early one winter morning I was huddled on a train platform in sub-zero temperatures with the rest of the commuters. I knew the drill. The train would arrive, and we would scurry aboard in the hopes of finding a seat so we didn't have to stand for the 40-minute trip into Grand Central Terminal.

(continued)

Standing on that platform I had the closest thing I've ever had to an epiphany. The people standing around me met every conventional measure of success, yet to maintain their affluent lifestyle required the long hours of commuting and high stress that come with well-paid jobs. It was part of the trade-off my fellow commuters had made. There's nothing wrong with that. It just wasn't what I wanted.

To me financial freedom was having options and not being tied down by obligations. My fear was that I would absentmindedly meander into a life I didn't want through what I'll call lifestyle creep. If I followed the conventional pathway, I would use each salary increase to fund more fixed obligations, like a bigger mortgage or higher car repayments. Each new obligation would move me further away from my definition of financial freedom.

This story illustrates how we craft narratives to order our lives. Those narratives may be truthful, but they don't necessarily contain the whole truth. This one captures a critical moment in the development of my money philosophy, but it doesn't capture each of the steps along the way.

My aversion to spending money on stuff, encapsulated in my revelation on the train platform, was not born of some profound rejection of materialism. First it was about not having enough money and letting myself feel okay about that. Part of that was just being young, but I also had closed off opportunities to make more money early in my career by not taking university more seriously. It took me a while and I had to get a graduate degree before my career started to take off.

Right after university I didn't earn much, and in retrospect I recognise this drove a lot of insecurity, which manifested in a strange way. I assumed an air of moral superiority by not buying things, avoiding debt at all costs, and saving and investing everything I could. Did this make me a better person? Of course not. It just allowed me to feel better about myself.

My efforts would be hidden away in my investment accounts and not put on display by having a nice apartment, nice things or enviable experiences. In retrospect I understand that because I couldn't compete in a traditional way I rejected the conventional approach to life. And in a way this reflected what got me into this situation — my rejection of the conventional approach of putting a modicum of effort into my university studies.

While I was being self-righteous about my spending and savings, I did learn some things. I've always been reserved and shy, and one of the advantages of a life spent gravitating to the sidelines is the opportunity to observe others. I went to private schools and grew up in wealthy communities, and many of my peers came from privileged backgrounds. Most of them had more success early in their careers than I did. I watched what they did with their salaries.

I watched them strive to replicate the trappings of the life they had known before they were in a position to pay for it themselves. As a society we don't talk about the financial foundations that underpin wealth. It is considered crass to talk directly about money so it should be no surprise that many people believe that projecting the illusion of wealth is the same as having it.

I saw a familiar pattern among my friends. Each pay increase was used not as an opportunity to become more financially secure but to finance a better lifestyle. This often entailed increased borrowing. Higher salaries perversely made them less financially secure and independent. The ubiquity of available credit meant that more income increased borrowing power, and many of them jumped at it.

(continued)

Projecting wealth was the priority; building wealth was not. None of this was done deliberately. It just seemed to be a default pattern they fell into because they didn't think about their money philosophy. This is very common. Before many people figure out what they want in life they start to reduce the financial flexibility that will allow them to pivot when they do. There is a difference between frivolous one-time spending and entering into longer-term obligations. We often see the latter as preferable, as these obligations typically fund the purchase of assets. However, without sufficient foresight such spending can block the achievement of future goals.

This approach to life works well, until it doesn't. When we are early in our careers, we tend to have many opportunities to make more money even if our salary growth is off a low base. Getting additional degrees, more certifications and more experience often leads to better pay, yet over time this diminishes. There are a variety of reasons for this, but all of us reach a point where our earning capacity plateaus. This point is often only clear in retrospect. Some people move into high-paying roles later in life, which more than makes up for early financial mistakes and obligations. But many don't.

While I wasn't making much money, I could see how each tiny improvement in my living standard quickly transformed something I wanted into something I needed. We get used to new things very quickly and they become hard to give up.

Lifestyle creep and using salary increases to fund higher future obligations looked to me like a trap. I started thinking about my salary and spending differently. I wanted my salary increases to go towards buying assets that further increased my future cash flows. I didn't want them to fund borrowing to buy assets that reduced future cash flows and didn't bring me joy. In my case, this included a house or a car.

I wanted to reduce the amount of each pay cheque that went to fixed obligations like housing, transport and healthcare. I wanted more of that cheque to go to discretionary spending that could be directed towards things that made me happy. There is of course nothing wrong with wanting or needing a house or a car. The key is to understand the risk and financial ramifications of stretching to afford something beyond your means.

Perhaps part of my attitude was my natural contrarian streak. If what everyone else was doing seemed like a trap, I would do the opposite. Yet it also seemed to make a lot more sense than traditional budgeting advice. Budgeting is about giving things up to accomplish a goal. And that is hard because giving up things we've become accustomed to is hard. I chose never to get used to them in the first place.

I also rejected the arbitrary one-size-fits-all advice on spending contained in many budgeting guides that prescribes that a certain percentage of spending be allocated to wants and another to needs. Even worse than blindly following such advice is the outsourcing of such decisions. The bank tells you how much house you can afford. The car dealer tells you how much car you can afford. They don't care about you. They will lend as much money as possible so long as they believe you will pay it back. None of this made any sense to me.

One big influence on my finances when I was building my financial philosophy was that Haley was not earning any money as she pursued her PhD studies. By necessity we were a single income household. We could only afford the lifestyle my salary could provide. By the time Haley started to earn money, we had already developed our financial philosophy. We had already decided on the life we wanted to live. This turned out to be a blessing.

(continued)

We didn't use her pay to further our lifestyle and instead saved her entire salary. We had been forced to live on a single salary and now we chose to continue to do so. We had to be very careful, but we managed.

Lifestyle creep is not just the process of spending more as you earn more. It is the process of structuring your spending and personal finances mindlessly and falling into a life that is not aligned with what makes you happy. A definition of 'creep' is to move slowly and carefully to avoid being noticed, and this is something that tends to happen in our financial lives.

I thought I had it all figured out. We were saving a large percentage of our income, and ridiculously, I had decided that in doing so, I was better than other people. What I hadn't spent too much time thinking about was the purpose of all my savings. Yes, it was for things like retirement, but I hadn't yet made the leap to seeing my finances as an enabler of the life I wanted to live. Strangely, I would learn this lesson through my obsessive saving.

I started saving for tuition for my children through a tax-advantaged account in the US called a 529 plan. The fact that I didn't have any children inexplicably played no role in this decision. My fixation on saving was so strong that I was literally inventing new reasons to save. All I could think about was getting rid of a future expense so I would have more options later in life.

Years later Haley and I made the decision not to have children. Even I couldn't invent a rationale to save and invest for non-existent children. I obviously could have taken the money and just added it to other investment accounts. However, I had finally come to the conclusion that I was letting life pass me by. My frugality was causing me to miss too many experiences. I didn't care about the apartment I was living in. I didn't want more stuff. I did want to travel and experience the world.

I took the money and opened a separate investment account and decided to spend the dividends on travel. At first this dividend income was very small. In the first year it would pay for part of a flight to a domestic location. The friends I told about this thought I was crazy. They couldn't understand why I wouldn't save less and just buy the flight. Yet it made sense to me. I was growing my passive income stream, and my investment income finally had a tangible impact on my life. It encouraged me to keep saving when I was starting to experience savings fatigue.

As my travel income stream started to grow it was a tangible example of how my investments could contribute to my life. Not in the future. Right now.

This was the final component of my money philosophy. Life is about more than investments. Investments are a means to an end. The end result I wanted was to live my life in a way that maximised my happiness, so I needed to judge financial success in those terms.

Adding another zero to my net worth didn't directly contribute to my happiness. It was too abstract. All saving and investing involves delayed gratification. You give and give and give with the prospect of getting something back years into the future. That is why it is so hard to sustain. For me, to keep going meant I wanted to get something back now.

Shani's money philosophy

My parents lived comfortable lives in Sri Lanka. Both were well-educated and had supportive families. They had friends and a sense of community. They were established in life, my dad just short of forty and my mum in her early thirties, when we moved to Australia.

My parents uprooted their lives and spent much of their savings to come to Australia in exchange for better opportunities for my sister and me. Migrating to a new country later in life involves trading all that is familiar for the insecurity of trying to learn a new culture, new norms and new rules. Assimilation is a gradual and challenging process. This was the environment I grew up in and it has left an indelible mark on all aspects of my life, including my relationship with money. Financial stability was the family priority when I was growing up and was core to my parents' approach to money and saving. The only financial products I was exposed to were residential housing and cash.

The lessons I took from my childhood were to seek stability and follow a conventional path. Unsurprisingly, this extended to my attitude and approach to money. It was not to be put at risk and was not to be spent frivolously. This has manifested itself in my continuing inability to spend money on myself while having few qualms about spending it on loved ones.

Given my childhood, it should come as no surprise that investing did not come naturally to me. My investing journey involved the usual steps of studying different concepts and ping-ponging between various approaches. I made some mistakes and learned some valuable lessons from those mistakes.

More than anything my investing journey has been a battle between my brain and my gut. My gut is driven by all the subconscious lessons from my childhood with the singular message: play it safe. My brain is driven by the lessons I've learned since working in the financial services industry. I've had to impose my money philosophy on myself over the objections of ... me.

There is no way to reason away your feelings. I know this because I've tried. When I first started investing I tried to invest the way my colleagues did. They were always looking for the next investment whose performance chart looked like a hockey stick to the sky. It was a sport, and they used the access they had to analysts, portfolio managers and institutional data to try to create wealth for themselves. This wasn't for me. Over time I have worked my way through the common mistakes investors make that are sometimes propagated by the industry in which I work. My money philosophy has evolved as I have come to know myself better as an investor and to understand what is important to me in life and what I want to achieve.

I've found that adding rigid structures to my savings has led to success for me. I have amounts for investing set aside as non-negotiables and I increase this with each promotion or pay rise. My superannuation is set up to help me achieve the outcomes I want. Compulsory contributions are going into it through my employer (and my salary sacrifice) on a regular basis, regardless of what is happening with the market. I've lifted this structure and behaviour for my investments outside of superannuation in order to avoid the temptation to allocate tactically, which would involve changing my approach based on my perception of market conditions.

What motivates me to save and invest and what underpins my money philosophy is independence. I never want to be controlled financially, whether in a relationship or in a workplace. Having money means others cannot exert control over me. Before I even felt the urge to invest I knew this was

(continued)

something I wanted in my life. I think it is a common goal for many people.

My money philosophy has been shaped by my life experiences. Over time I've figured out what is important to me. Financial independence is the foundation of my money philosophy. Later in this book I will recount my realisation that investing has the potential to open up possibilities for what I can achieve in my life. However, these goals will always be secondary to achieving independence. And I am lucky that I have the ability to plan for more than that.

I'm really excited about the opportunities I have to live the life I want, but I do feel guilty. My life looks very different from those of my mum and dad or many of my relatives in Sri Lanka. Close family members weren't able to get a passport because of poor government documentation, so they never saw beyond their bubble. I don't think this guilt is uncommon among first-generation migrants. It is a reaction to knowing that the opportunity afforded to me is a result of my parents' move to Australia. They did this so I could have a better life even if it made their own lives more challenging. I have choices about my financial future, what I can achieve and what I want to do. These choices are enabled by making smart choices with money, valuing frugality, always looking to the future and making sure I consider all opportunities wisely.

Key takeaways

A financial philosophy is a foundational set of beliefs and values that drive your interactions with money. Financial freedom means different things for everyone. Your journey starts with defining what is important for you and creating a narrative to guide your decision making.

The secret to success is alignment between your money worldview, what you want to achieve and your plan to accomplish your goal. The foundation is a financial philosophy that ensures your saving and investing goals are clear and that you know how your financial resources will support the life you want to live. Everyone needs to invest to get ahead. Your financial philosophy is why *you* need to invest, what you are trying to achieve and, potentially, what negative mindsets you need to overcome.

The maths behind financial freedom

There is an inescapable truth behind your finances. The maths matter. We know that is not what most people want to hear. According to Stanford University professor Jo Boaler, up to 50 per cent of the population have maths anxiety. There is going to be some maths in this book. We promise it won't be that bad.

Everyone has unique goals and circumstances, so there is no one-size-fits-all approach to investing. This means the maths won't always lead to the right course of action. We can't stress that point too strongly. The goal is not to become a robot that always follows the path that maximises wealth; it is to get what you want out of life and have your finances play an enabling role. In saying that, however, it's still necessary to do the maths. If you don't, you won't be able to make an informed decision because you won't have a basis from which to figure out what is right for you.

A logical place to start is with the concept that is central to building wealth — compounding. In chapter 1 we talked about doubling your wealth. The secret to that is compounding. Every investing commentator is talking about compounding. Some even understand how it works. Soon you will too.

Einstein reportedly called compound interest the 'eighth wonder of the world'. At a basic level compounding is earning a return on a return. That simple definition has a lot of implications for how you should invest.

Exercise: Mark and Shani's compounding quiz #1

Compounding is not as simple as it is often portrayed. This quiz will uncover how the concept of compounding is applied in real life. We will go through the maths at the end of the chapter.

Here's the base case for each question: if you were to invest $10 000 annually for 40 years and earn a 7 per cent return, you would end up with $2.136 million from your $400 000 investment. Not too bad. See whether you can answer the following questions based on this scenario:

1. If you stopped saving for the last 20 years and just earned the 7 per cent annual return on total savings of $200 000 what percentage of the $2.136 million would you end up with?

    a. 50 per cent

    b. 20 per cent

    c. 80 per cent

    d. 60 per cent

2. If you delayed saving by 20 years and saved and invested $200 000 over the remaining 20 years of the original period what percentage of the $2.136 million would you end up with?

    a. 50 per cent

    b. 20 per cent

    c. 80 per cent

    d. 60 per cent

3. You still earned a 7 per cent average annual return over the full 40-year period but instead of earning 7 per cent each year you earned a 4 per cent return over the first 20 years and a 10 per cent return over the last 20 years. What percentage of the $2.136 million would you end up with?

    a. Same amount

    b. 125 per cent

    c. 80 per cent

    d. 70 per cent

4. You earned a 7 per cent annual return over the full 40-year period but instead of earning 7 per cent each year you earned a 10 per cent annual return over the first 20 years and a 4 per cent annual return over the last 20 years. What percentage of the $2.136 million would you end up with?

    a. Same amount

    b. 125 per cent

    c. 80 per cent

    d. 70 per cent

The answers to these questions have implications for the approach you should take with saving and investing. Being able to answer the questions is the difference between truly understanding compounding and just knowing the definition.

The maths behind compounding

While the term is thrown around in investing circles ad nauseam, there is a difference between knowing something and understanding it. In this chapter we aim to foster understanding of the implications of compounding for building wealth.

We are going to use the same base case from the quiz. For 40 years $10 000 is saved annually and a 7 per cent return is earned each year. The savings are steady, which doesn't align with a growing salary and savings over a career. The return is steady, which obviously does not correlate with how volatile markets work. But the example illustrates the impact of compounding.

Compounding can be very powerful, which is why it is frequently cited in investing commentary. In 40 years a total of $400 000 saved and invested turns into $2.136 million in wealth.

When we break down the 40-year period of saving and investing several lessons from compounding are uncovered. In the first year 93 per cent of the wealth created comes from savings and only 7 per cent from market returns. In the last year of the 40-year period the opposite occurs. Savings only account for 7 per cent of the total wealth gain, with 93 per cent coming from market returns.

This is compounding lesson number one. When you are young every dollar saved has a huge impact on future outcomes. When you are older savings don't matter as much. What matters are returns. However, these two observations are related. Returns have such a large impact late in life *because* you saved early.

The implication is that it is very hard to catch up when you are older, no matter how much you save. It is never too late to take control of your finances and start your journey to financial freedom, yet each day counts as time you can never retrieve. Understanding compounding is understanding the maths behind the oft-repeated phrase that the best time to start was yesterday and the next best time is today.

The idea of starting early contrasts with the way many people approach their finances. They don't worry about saving and investing when they are young because they tell themselves they will make up for it later when they 'make more money'.

We can demonstrate the advantage of starting early by adjusting the baseline scenario. In this case we can explore what happens if savings stopped after the first 20 years. You end up with total wealth of $1.697 million. Although only half as much was saved, 80 per cent of the total wealth was still created over the 40 years.

To reinforce this point, we can consider the opposite scenario. In this case, our hypothetical investor did not start saving and investing in the first 20 years and ended up with $438 652. Once again half as much was saved, but in this case only 20 per cent of the total wealth from the base case was created.

What is the impact of different return scenarios?

We can now highlight the impact from different sequences or orders of returns. The steady returns in the base case of 7 per cent a year ignores the inherent volatility of the market. In the real world, in some years or even for stretches of years the sharemarket does great. In others it doesn't.

If instead of steady returns a 4 per cent return was earned over the first 20 years and 10 per cent over the last 20 years things change dramatically. Over the full 40-year period the average return is exactly the same as if the return had been 7 per cent every year but the total wealth generated is \$2.713 million. In this case, total wealth was more than 25 per cent higher than our base case.

The opposite occurs if we reverse that scenario. The average return remains exactly the same but 10 per cent returns were earned over the first 20 years and 4 per cent over the last 20 years. Total wealth created has now dropped from the base case by 20 per cent.

Unfortunately we don't get to pick when markets do well or poorly. For each person who is lucky to be born at the right time someone else is unlucky. However, if you had to pick you would want the highest returns later in life. As was demonstrated in the first example, later in life is when returns matter more and savings matter less. Conversely, retiring after a bear market is challenging.

Mark says...

A financial calculator allows you to play around with different inputs and see the impact on your future wealth. You can adjust the returns, how much you invest and the time you invest, and out pops a new future value. I'm not proud of this, but when I first got a financial calculator, in my early twenties, I couldn't stop playing with it. I would come up with different scenarios and see the impact of saving more, earning a higher return and investing for longer. This gave me a real appreciation that time was my most valuable resource. It made me aware that saving a little bit in my twenties would have the same impact as saving a lot when I was older. I'm glad I figured that out early, because now I don't need to save as aggressively.

Exercise: Mark and Shani's compounding quiz #2

The answers to the following quiz questions should be clearer after you've gone through the maths of compounding:

1. If you stopped saving 20 years ago and just earned market returns on total savings of $200 000, what percentage of the $2.136 million would you end up with? The answer is 80 per cent.

2. If you delayed saving by 20 years and saved and invested $200 000 over the remaining 20 years of the original period, what percentage of the $2.136 million would you end up with? The answer is 20 per cent.

3. You still earned a 7 per cent annual return over the full 40-year period but instead of earning 7 per cent each year you earned a 4 per cent annual return over the first 20 years and 10 per cent over the last 20 years. What percentage of the $2.136 million would you end up with? The answer is 125 per cent.

4. You earned a 7 per cent annual return over the full 40-year period but instead of earning 7 per cent each year you earned a 10 per cent annual return over the first 20 years and 4 per cent over the last 20 years. What percentage of the $2.136 million would you end up with? The answer is 80 per cent.

So what are the implications of the maths behind compounding?

Wasting time is a terrible thing

The last thing we want to do is preach to young investors. We know that youth is portrayed as the time to take risks, to try new things, take time out to experience life — and perhaps go after speculative investments.

We have nothing against this. Just keep your eyes wide open about the trade-offs you are making. From a financial perspective, time is your most valuable asset. Understanding compounding means knowing there is an opportunity cost to delaying saving and investing.

We do have something against speculative investments. Take a punt and lose $10000 on a speculative investment in year 5 of the 40-year timeframe and it isn't $10000 you need to earn back; it's a bit more than $114000 by year 40. Blow $10000 on some extravagant purchase that doesn't bring joy to your life and the result is the same. Your mindset matters. What you are spending and what you are risking on some speculative bet matters a lot more when you are young. Lose $10000 in year 35 and all that's needed to make it back is a bit over $14000 by year 40.

Obviously $10000 is a significantly smaller portion of total wealth at the end of this hypothetical 40-year scenario. Yet what remains true is that squandering money when you are young is not just about the money. What is really being squandered is time, your most valuable investing resource.

Compounding means wealth generation accelerates over time

Halfway through the 40-year period of our baseline scenario the total wealth generated is less than 19 per cent of the total at the end of the period. In the last five years 44 per cent of the total portfolio value is generated. Compounding takes time — you need to be patient and not give up.

No-one better illustrates this than Warren Buffett. In his great book *The Psychology of Money*, Morgan Housel points out how 99 per cent of Buffett's wealth was generated after he was 65.

More than anything this demonstrates that the best way to take advantage of compounding is by waiting. This can be hard because progress in the beginning is slow and hard to see, but it accelerates dramatically as you approach your goal.

Course correcting later in life is hard

Persuading someone to focus on retirement at the beginning of their career is challenging. Luckily in Australia we have compulsory employer contributions into super, but some workers, such as the self-employed, don't fall under the mandate. According to the Association of Superannuation Funds of Australia (ASFA), 20 per cent of self-employed Australians don't have any superannuation.

Self-employed Aussies who do have a balance were likely employed at some point in their working life. Only 30 per cent of those aged 60–64 have more than $100 000 in their super. The truth is, we all tend to procrastinate and focus on the immediate challenges we face, but this tendency makes things harder later in life.

Compounding is a powerful driver for building wealth. The proof of that power is how difficult it is to course correct as timeframes get shorter. We can demonstrate this by modifying one of the scenarios we have explored.

Saving for only the last 20 years of the 40-year timeframe results in a significantly lower level of wealth than saving for the first 20 years or for the entire period. For example, what will an investor who has not saved for the first half of the 40-year time period need to do to achieve the wealth that would have been hers had she begun saving $10 000 a year 20 years earlier? Assuming the same return of 7 per cent per year, she would need to save $48 696 a year from year 20 to year 40.

Starting to save and invest early enables more options later in life, and these options accelerate financial freedom. In this case, an investor who starts early will have close to $39 000 more to spend each year later in life. Even small amounts of savings can make a big difference when we add the element of time.

Shani says...

The maths behind investing is important. It provides a logical path for your decision making in what can be an emotional endeavour. At the foundation of my approach is understanding the maths behind long-term investing. I know that asset allocation is the largest contributor to returns. I know that if I invest $100 and I'm able to save and contribute $10 more, I will have $110. That is effectively the same as a 10 per cent return from the market, but it is entirely within my control. I understand how reinvesting my income is key to building wealth through compounding. The logic of investing and how it works is what makes the risk worth it in the end. It is the basis of every decision I make in my portfolio.

Savings and investments are not the only things that compound

In an investing context, we always think of compounding as a good thing. It's how we turn small amounts of money into large sums by simply adding the element of time. Wealth is not the only thing that compounds.

Compounding of fees

Because compounding is such a powerful driver of wealth creation, we want to do everything possible to make sure we don't reduce its impact. Many people don't appreciate the impact of fees on wealth generation.

We can turn to Australia's largest superfund as an example. The annual fees on a $250 000 balance in AustralianSuper's pre-mixed options are $1727. That is 0.69 per cent. If you remove the annual $302 admin fee, the remaining investment management fees represent 0.57 per cent of the total account balance.

The AustralianSuper fees include admin, transaction costs and investment fees. This is low for a super fund, but 0.57 per cent for transaction and investment fees is still high in an absolute sense. If you saved $10 000 for 40 years and earned a return of 9.04 per cent, you would end up with $3.415 million. If the fees are added back in, the return would be 9.61 per cent and you would have $3.981 million. That is a huge difference.

If you invest $10 000 a year for 40 years and grow those contributions to $3.015 million, over a lifetime you will pay AustralianSuper a staggering $566 000. More on fees later.

Compounding of debt

We live in an age of abundant credit. And the companies trying to sell us stuff have an advantage over the average consumer. The companies understand compounding, and most consumers don't. Almost any purchase can be transformed magically from a lump sum a consumer would balk at paying into an apparently affordable monthly payment.

This magical transformation involves interest that negatively compounds a $1000 couch into a $2000 couch. Every magic trick needs a flourish to distract the audience from what is actually happening. In this case, it is the combination of the emotional rush we experience when we buy stuff and the affordable monthly payment. The advent and popularity of the buy-now-pay-later option is a perfect example of this. The average balance of a buy-now-pay-later account as of July 2024 was $867 with an interest rate between 0 and 36 per cent, with the effective interest rate being as high as 177.44 per cent for a $40 purchase with late fees.

Many of the goods and services we consume involve emotions. It isn't just a suit or a dress. It is the way you will look and feel in that suit or dress during a big job interview or on a special date. This same emotional pull influences our purchasing decisions, for example on vacations, cars and houses — items often funded with borrowed money.

Purchasing certain items requires borrowing money. Houses and cars are the most obvious example. Everyone needs a place to live, and a car is a necessity for many people. We are not suggesting you don't borrow to finance either purchase. Just remember that when emotions are combined with seemingly affordable monthly payments, we can lose sight of the real cost. Stretching your budget for a certain house or adding some features to a car can cost far more than we think.

Exercise: On compounding

Now you understand compounding a little better it's time to contemplate how you will use compounding to help you achieve financial freedom. The maths behind compounding is universal. However, the best approach to take will differ depending, for example, on your goal and your age.

Think about the upsides of compounding and the interplay between savings and returns. Consider the negative impacts of compounding, how fees can compound, and how taxes and other costs break the momentum of compounding.

Write down a few bullet points on how compounding can help you achieve financial freedom.

Following are some general considerations for different age groups that you might want to adapt to your personal circumstances. Remember, the purpose of this book is to show you how to develop your own personal financial plan. One-size-fits-all approaches to money just don't work. Later we will outline the ways that compounding can help you decide on your investment strategy.

When you're just starting out

Time is the investor's most valuable resource. Don't give it up easily. The tax savings from superannuation compound over time. Save in super first to take advantage of as many years of low taxes as possible. This will free up more of your financial resources later in life so you can direct them towards other goals instead of desperately trying to catch up. The longer money can compound, the more valuable it will be. So try to save as much as you can when you are younger. Also do what you can to avoid speculative investments, paying capital gains taxes from trading too much or paying high fees.

Given the long timeline, the impact of every good thing you do, like saving money, and every bad thing you do, like paying fees or taxes, is amplified.

It is also critical not to give up. Progress will initially seem slow, because you have smaller account balances. It may seem inconceivable that such a small pot of money will grow into such a large one, but incremental progress and the magic of compounding will get you there. Spend some time thinking about the different scenarios we went through earlier in this chapter to understand how compounding works, and have faith that over time you will reach your goal.

When you're in mid to late career

At this point, returns are playing a bigger role in your outcome. There's little you can do about the overall return levels of the market, but you can focus on the things that detract from returns, such as by minimising fees and taxes.

Later we will consider the biggest influence on returns—poor investor behaviour—and the structures you can put in place to minimise mistakes.

It's also worth considering the best use of your savings. If you've taken care of your retirement early, you may have other options when it comes to directing savings. One place is to eliminate expenses such as paying off your mortgage. This may be a better use for your savings later in life as you are approaching the end of your mortgage.

When compounding hit home for Shani

I'm amazed looking back to when I thought a fund with a management fee of more than 1 per cent was normal. I worked at a fund manager with active funds and ETFs, so I invested in active funds and ETFs. As competition has increased the fund industry has cut fees. Yet the fees I was paying were still excessive. I somehow rationalised the fee in my head by virtue of the strong track record of the funds.

Like Mark, I started to play around with financial calculators. I focused on the variables that impacted returns. Moneysmart (a government website) has a great calculator that provides a visualisation of your total return along with the impact of fees.

Imagine a scenario in which you have $100 000 invested and contribute $1000 a month. You earn a 7 per cent return per year over 20 years. Table 3.1 shows what your account balance will look like, depending on your fund's fee levels.

Table 3.1: the impact of fees on your account balance

Fee p.a. (%)	Account balance ($)	Fees paid ($)
1.50	711 940	182 565
1.00	767 603	126 902
0.75	797 293	97 212
0.50	828 298	66 206
0.25	860 681	33 824
0.05	887 622	6 883

What stood out to me was that the fee doesn't proportionately decrease. This is *reverse compounding.*

I started to do the maths and saw that I was paying a fee for something that more than likely won't outperform a passive product that is a fraction of the price. This is not to say that all active management is bad. However, for a lot of the exposure I was looking for, my research showed that most active managers underperformed once the higher fees were taken into account.

Fees are not the only consideration when you're picking an investment product, but the maths shows it should be front of mind.

(continued)

The concept of reverse compounding doesn't just relate to fees. You can apply it to anything that will detract from your returns. Debt is impacted as the interest you pay compounds.

A 2024 study by Vanguard Australia showed that exercises like this really help investors. Superannuation accounts are particularly sticky. We tend to be lazy and would rather not go through the hassle of switching. The study found that half of Australians said they'd never switched their superfund. When they saw the difference switching could make to their retirement outcomes, however, 72 per cent considered taking action.

Understanding the variables that impact your total return will make you a better investor. It will help you to improve your outcomes as you make the necessary trade-offs between fees and value.

How Mark learned the importance of understanding the maths behind investing

I hated maths class when I was at school. Part of the reason I hated it was because I thought I was terrible at it. When I was trying to work in the financial industry I took a series of exams to earn the CFA (Chartered Financial Analyst) qualification. The exams involved a good deal of anxiety-creating maths.

Yet as I was studying it all started making more sense. I've come to see that the way maths is presented in school has little to do with the real world. In school a maths problem has all the data needed to solve an equation. There's a single right answer.

In the real world there's little need to calculate anything. We have calculators and computers for that. And you don't have all the information to solve a problem, so there's often no single right answer.

This became clear to me as I studied for the CFA exams. I wanted to understand the maths behind financial decisions, not because it would tell me exactly what to do, but because not understanding would mean I would never know what to do. Real maths is not about calculations. It is about being numerically literate so you are better able to solve problems.

I know a lot of readers probably also believe they aren't any good at maths. That belief is likely holding them back when it comes to managing their finances. I encourage you to reframe what maths is and give it another shot. The problem is likely not about you but about your experiences with maths.

Key takeaways

Understand how the maths of compounding can inform decision making, including the impact of time on wealth generation and the risk of breaking or slowing the compounding cycle.

Among the hardest things about investing is staying consistent over decades and minimising mistakes. Writing down the principles of compounding that apply to your goals and circumstances can serve as a reminder of the long-term drivers of wealth generation. This will be a key input into your personalised investment strategy.

Investors behaving badly

Chapter 3 explained the maths behind investing. The message is clear. Compounding is the key to achieving your financial goals, and anything that disrupts compounding reduces your ability to achieve your goals. And poor investor behaviour is the biggest disruptor of effective compounding.

Benjamin Graham was one of the most influential investors. He was Warren Buffett's professor at Columbia Business School and his first employer at Graham–Newman Corp. He professionalised the investment industry and authored one of the most famous and influential books on investing... you get the point.

The Intelligent Investor (1949) is not exactly a page-turner, unless you really like reading about railroad bonds. Graham was a deep-value investor, which involved analysing the financial statements of companies in detail. He was ahead of his time in recognising that investing was not simply a rational assessment of the prospects of different investments. He famously said, 'The investor's chief problem — and even his worst enemy — is likely to be himself.'

The Intelligent Investor was partly an analytical exploration of valuing companies, but it was also an exploration of the impact of emotions on the investing process. His personification of investor behaviour, Mr Market, is prone to alternating bouts of euphoria and pessimism and is sometimes willing to pay exorbitant prices for companies and, sometimes, just as willing to sell them for a fraction of their value.

Graham's work was ground-breaking because he intuited what would come to seem obvious. He had no data to support the impact of poor investor behaviour, but he observed the role emotions played in investment decisions, generally to the detriment of investors.

He published his book *The Intelligent Investor* in 1949. It was in the age of classical economics when the prevailing orthodoxy was that humans behave rationally. The assumption of rationality was convenient for economists because discounting emotions made it easy to model the economic impact of different policies. The inconvenient part of this assumption is that it isn't true.

The field of behavioural economics was pioneered in the 1970s by psychologists Amos Tversky and Daniel Kahneman. Their research into the ways humans fail to act rationally revolutionised how we think about investor behaviour. By uncovering the ways we don't act rationally they unlocked the secrets to making better decisions. Before we get to this we need to explore just how much investors sabotage themselves.

Reassess your image of a successful investor

If there is a common theme through this book, it is that the portrayal of successful investing is wrong. This means the way most people go about investing is wrong. We are presented with a narrative about successful investing that openly mocks the impact of humility, consistency and patience when it comes to outcomes. But we argue that these characteristics may be the secrets to success.

We are told that the key to success is action. Successful investors nimbly and confidently adjust their portfolios to take advantage of every twist and turn in the economy. Geopolitical uncertainty is an opportunity. Buy and hold is dead.

As we've pointed out, a cynic might suggest that this misleading portrayal is deliberate, since lots of people profit from this picture of successful investing. More trading is good for brokers. The constant turnover benefits product providers who introduce more and more thematic and niche ways to invest with management fees that far exceed the vanilla options.

If it is all too overwhelming, you can just pay somebody else to manage your money. To be a financial expert today means always having an opinion on what to do. There are no points for advising a client that the best course of action is to do nothing. The lesson is that you should always have an opinion on what to do, and there is no point in having an opinion if you don't act on it.

We know most investors think success comes from constant activity. This isn't just a result of how we've been conditioned. It is also instinctual. Deeply ingrained in all humans is a survival instinct based on fight or flight. Faced with a predator, do you fight, or do you run?

Watching markets surge or plunge elicits an emotional response. Money isn't just money. Embedded in each tick of a portfolio higher or lower is a sense of security, status and hopes for the future. We don't just want to act; we feel the *need* to act. This happens constantly. There is always going to be new data, an articulate advocate for a certain action, or a price fluctuation that triggers fear or greed.

Investors have given in to the combination of external reinforcement that action leads to success and our inbuilt action bias. The World Economic Forum reported that in June 2020 the average holding period of a share trading on the New York Stock Exchange (NYSE) was five and a half months, down from 14 months in 2019. The average holding period has been dropping for decades after reaching a high of close to eight years in the mid 1960s. There is little evidence that all this trading has done anything but enrich the industry and harm investors.

It may sound counterintuitive but the best thing to do in almost every environment is to take no action and stick to your plan. The problem is that most investors don't have a plan. You will not be one of those investors after you have finished reading this book.

To succeed at anything means finding your competitive advantage and focusing on exploiting that advantage as best you can. Any investor can gain an advantage by simply controlling behaviour. It really is as simple as controlling your own actions. As Benjamin Graham perceived so many years ago, the problem is us.

What is good behaviour?

The blueprint for achieving financial freedom that we've laid out aims to prevent the mistakes that sabotage far too many people who are trying to improve their lives. To change someone's behaviour, you first need to convince that person they are not acting in their own best interests. We will do that by referencing several studies. Bear with us.

At Morningstar we conduct an annual survey called 'Mind the Gap'. It looks at the difference between the returns in the underlying investments such as funds and ETFs and the returns the end investor actually receives. The difference is based on timing decisions — when investors purchased and sold the funds and ETFs.

While the results vary from year to year, the conclusion is the same: investors underperform the investments in their portfolio. In the 2024 survey, that underperformance was 1.60 per cent per year.

Take a minute to ponder these findings. We are constantly told that what matters is the investment products we have in our portfolio. The implications are clear. If what matters is what is in our portfolio, we should always make sure we hold the best investments. Enter market commentators who will tell you what the best investments are based on whatever is happening in the world. Yet in reality we are not being hurt by not holding the 'right' investment. We are hurting ourselves by constantly trying to find that 'right' investment. We have met the enemy... and it is us.

How much is this impacting our results? A lot. According to Vanguard's 2024 Index Chart, Australian shares have delivered returns of 9.10 per cent a year for the past 30 years. If you had invested $10 000 a year for 30 years and earned a 9.10 per cent return, you would now have $1.388 million. Subtract 1.60 per cent from those returns and you end up with $1.033 million. In this scenario investors would have 25 per cent less money simply by constantly trying to find the 'right' investments.

Other studies have shown the same impact. Professors Brad Barber and Terrance Odean at the University of California have undertaken multiple studies into investor behaviour. One famous study from 1999, 'Do Investors Trade Too Much?', used

US brokerage account data to look at times when investors sold one investment to purchase another. This is typical investment behaviour, as something needs to be sold to fund the purchase of a great new idea. The problem is that the great new ideas typically aren't so great. Odean and Barber found that the investment sold outperformed the one that was purchased by an average of 3.32 per cent after 504 trading days.

The research is clear. When the typical investor makes a trade, investing results get worse. Logically this means that investors who trade more don't do as well as investors who trade less, and it turns out there are lots of studies that show this logic stands up to scrutiny.

In 'Trading Is Hazardous to Your Wealth', published in 2000, Odean and Barber divided investors across quintiles by the amount they traded. Net monthly returns (which include costs) for each quintile were as follows:

- Highest trading quintile = 1.01 per cent per month
- Second-highest trading quintile = 1.27 per cent per month
- Third-highest trading quintile = 1.36 per cent per month
- Fourth-highest trading quintile = 1.41 per cent per month
- Lowest trading quintile = 1.47 per cent per month.

The Morningstar study and the Odean and Barber studies looked at real-world data to explore the impact of investor behaviour.

The same behaviour shows up in simulations. An article by Batista and Massaro from 2017 (also titled 'Do Investors Trade Too Much?') looked at how investors behave in a controlled market.

The participants in the study were given cash and told they could choose when it would be invested in a stock that would increase in value, on average, by 2 per cent per time period. There were

100 time periods in the game. For each individual time period the stock's price moved up or down randomly, but it followed a pattern over longer periods, mirroring what happens in real markets. And just as in real markets, each transaction incurred a transaction cost.

Batista and Massaro confirmed that individuals tend to overtrade in an effort to beat the market or chase returns. Their analysis of the return outcomes at the end of the study showed that frequent trading eroded the gains as a result of poor timing and higher fees. The participants who adopted a buy-and-hold approach fared better across the board.

It seems easy enough to suggest that investors should simply trade less, but this doesn't address the reasons investors trade too frequently. Nobody is deliberately making poor decisions. In addition to your action bias there is a narrative around investing success that is contributing to poor behaviour. Following are some ways investors are led astray by commonly held notions of success.

1. Don't confuse competence with complexity

The bowerbird lives in Papua New Guinea and northern Australia. To attract a mate the male bowerbird builds an elaborate nest filled with brightly coloured objects. To choose a mate the female bird repeatedly visits different nests. During the visits the males put on a bit of a dance routine. The pressure is on the male birds. This is a winner-takes-all exercise since multiple females will choose to mate with the same male. Males with subpar nests and dance moves don't get to mate.

Seems simple enough. The female bird wants a nice place to raise her offspring, so she picks a male with a nice house. Plus some good dance moves never hurt anyone trying to mate. Perhaps a little shallow for our taste but you can't argue with the logic. Except the female bowerbird isn't a gold digger. The nest the male builds is just for show. After mating the male is out of the picture. The female builds another nest in which to lay her eggs and raise her young.

The bowerbirds who manically add more and more decorations to their nests aren't the only organisms that imagine add-ons to be the key to improvement. We humans have the same tendency. Conventional wisdom is that more is better. Professor Leidy Klotz explored this concept in his book *Subtract: The Untapped Science of Less.*

Klotz demonstrated that when asked to make something better, most people, like male bowerbirds, come up with the same solution — add more. To create a better Lego structure people added more Lego pieces. When asked to adjust an already jam-packed holiday itinerary people added more activities.

Most participants in Klotz's experiments never even considered subtraction as a solution. Subtraction is not always the best solution but to not even consider it is limiting. The 2023 'US Investor Study' by the firm Broadridge found that between 2018 and 2022 the average US investor increased the number of positions in their portfolios by 42 per cent. For 60-year-old investors the average portfolio contained 5.1 managed funds, 4.2 ETFs and 8.5 individual share holdings.

Investors are clearly comfortable with the adage that more is better. The fact that this meaningful increase in portfolio holdings occurred in conjunction with a proliferation of new investment products is unsurprising. As we've pointed out, the investment industry is incentivised to portray successful investing as complex because it encourages investors to pay for help managing their portfolios. It encourages more holdings and more trading, which is good for the industry. It is likely bad for investors.

There are benefits to simplicity when it comes to investing. This notion is explored by portfolio manager Ben Carson in his book *A Wealth of Common Sense*. He advises investors to create a buffer between their portfolios and their emotions, citing a study that shows people ate three times less chocolate if the sweets were a short walk away instead of just in front of them.

If your portfolio is simple you are likely to check it less often. Constantly checking your portfolio is the equivalent of having the chocolate right in front of you. You will be tempted to make frequent changes. Given investor predilections for chasing performance and overtrading at inopportune times, more changes are likely to result in lower returns. Decision fatigue may also set in; this refers to the deteriorating quality of decision making when constantly confronted with choices.

Diversification is important, but once you've achieved a certain level of diversification more holdings can be counterproductive. With broadly diversified ETFs you can build a portfolio with only a few holdings. You don't have to own every niche asset class.

The male bowerbirds compete to show competence, and even though that competence has no real-world value it succeeds in impressing female birds. We do this a lot as humans. We put on a show to impress people. Like that of the bowerbirds, the show bears little relation to actual competence.

Maybe you are the one responsible for investing for your family. Perhaps investing is also linked to your standing with your extended family and friends. You may be known as 'good with money'. Whether or not you intended this to happen, investing may have become part of your self-identity.

Perhaps your portfolio and investment strategy have become a bit like a bowerbird's nest. You have holdings that are in reality no more than brightly coloured ornaments that serve no practical purpose beyond representing your financial competence. The more complex your portfolio, the more competent you appear to your peers. You might sound smarter when describing your sophisticated portfolio at a cocktail party. You might also be hurting your long-term returns.

There are two ways to simplify your portfolio. The obvious way is to have fewer holdings. This probably means taking a passive approach. For many people that is sensible. Remember it takes no skill and little effort to get the average return. It takes more skill and more effort to try to beat the market, and most people fail. Average has a bad connotation in day-to-day life. But when it comes to investing, average is probably all you need to hit your goals.

The other way to simplify is to have a more straightforward investment strategy. Simple doesn't mean simplistic. For example, as she will explain, Shani's approach is to focus on controlling what she can control. This includes her savings levels, the fees she pays and her behaviour, all of which impact her tax outcomes. She lets her investments take care of themselves.

Mark also pursues a simple investment strategy though his approach to investing is more active than Shani's. He is an income investor and focuses on dividends with the goal of growing his passive income faster than inflation. It isn't that he doesn't care about capital appreciation. It just isn't his primary focus. This means not caring if his portfolio underperforms over multi-year periods. He just buys and holds great companies and ETFs and lets the dividends roll in.

Contrast Shani's and Mark's approaches with those of investors who are constantly trying to 'beat' the market. Such investors must worry about the macroeconomic environment, interest rates, geopolitical risks and the short-term catalysts for different types of investments. To do this means constantly monitoring their portfolio, forecasting short-term earnings, rotating their portfolio and continually re-evaluating each position. This is the way successful investing is portrayed in the media. It is also almost impossible to achieve. We think there is a real benefit to simplicity.

2. Be wary of copying professional investors

Michael Phelps spent six hours a day in the pool six days a week as he trained for the Olympics. He swam 13 kilometres a day fuelled by consuming 10 000 calories. This is an impressive training regime. It worked out pretty well for him.

No-one in their right mind would copy Phelps's approach to try to compete in, say, an adult swimming program. It is common sense that the training plan would be different for someone training for a gold medal in almost every event and someone trying to swim freestyle without running into the lane markers.

The same logic applies to investing. We will reiterate this concept constantly. You are not a professional investor. You have different goals. You have different resources. You have different ways of gaining a competitive advantage. Stop trying to mimic what professionals do, including both the way they invest and the investments they pick.

This goes for other individual investors as well. The overarching message of this book is that each person should design and follow a customised investing approach. An investment approach or a particular investment that works well for one person may not be right for another. Our goal is to help you create a plan tailored for you that instils the confidence to ignore the constant stream of advice from professional and individual investors whose goals are different from yours.

Mark says...

One of the best pieces of advice I ever got was that the more a person giving advice is different from you, the less useful the advice will be. That's how I feel about professional investors. I just don't think the way they invest has anything to do with the way I should invest. Their goals are different and the things that motivate and restrain them are different. There's a lot I can learn from them, but that doesn't mean I should invest in the ways they do. I think my behaviour is the single biggest driver of the outcomes I achieve. To get the best outcomes, I need to behave differently from most professionals.

---

3. Don't fall victim to hype

Capitalism is designed to foster competition. That competition becomes more intense as the level of growth increases. And competition is not something we relish as investors. We want to own companies that can fend off competitors and keep more of the spoils for shareholders. That's why we urge you to look for companies with a sustainable competitive advantage (or moat). Too often we lose sight of that investment principle in our Pavlovian response to growth. More on this later.

Competition means that capital chases growth. A company in a high-growth sector will be able to borrow with abandon. Venture capitalists, private equity and public market investors will battle to throw increasingly large piles of money at new and existing companies in high-growth sectors. You might be doing this.

The 'hot' areas of the economy are always talked about by the media. Investors get very excited about being part of the next big thing, but there's a downside. This infusion of capital creates more competition and often leads to poor outcomes for investors.

The way this plays out follows a pattern. At first everyone is happy as revenue growth is off the charts. Companies expand to meet untapped demand. Faster revenue growth leads to even more capital. Companies soak up capital like a sponge and they'll do anything to keep growing faster, lowering prices, increasing marketing and hiring more people to increase the production of goods and services. The companies become addicted to growth because their investors are addicted to growth.

It isn't long until we read about the amazing employee perks in these high-growth industries. Meals, facilities and offsites become increasingly lavish. The costs don't matter because there's always more money available to fund anything and everything. Profitability doesn't matter because that's tomorrow's problem. The name of the game is revenue growth.

Inevitably, challenges arise. Running a business is hard in any environment. Running a business in an environment with increasing competition with unlimited resources is even harder. At some point, supply will outstrip demand.

In a rational environment supply would be lowered. But the pressure to keep the party going is intense. Some companies will do dumb, short-sighted things that hurt them over the long term. Some will commit fraud. Whatever it takes. Between employees, investors and the media there are just too many cheerleaders who don't want the party to end.

Eventually things fall apart. Valuations collapse as investors finally catch on that the limitless future hawked by 'visionaries' might not be realistic. Some companies will fail. Some will be sold at fire-sale prices in a desperate bid at consolidation. Eventually a more rational competitive environment develops, but only after investors have lost lots of money.

Smart investors understand that the seeds of growth may be demand-based but that eventually they sprout into an abundance of supply. Others continue to chase the next new and exciting investments, driven by the fear of missing out.

Shani says...

Like all investors, I made mistakes before coming to my approach. I've tried to learn from these mistakes to become a better investor and improve my future outcomes. My behaviour is one of the core reasons I take the approach I do, and this has informed my investment strategy and the type of investments I hold. My investment strategy may not be maximising outcomes, but it is maximising *my* outcomes. It reduces the temptation to overtrade, to chase after hot investments and to sell out at the bottom of the market.

Case Study: The junk-bond king and the danger of hype

There are countless historical examples of when hype and a compelling-sounding narrative have captivated investors. One example comes from the junk-bond bubble and crash in the 1980s. A young Michael Milken read W Braddock Hickman's *Corporate Bond Quality and Investor Experience* when he was at university.

Milken latched on to one of Braddock's conclusions: that a well-diversified portfolio of low-grade bonds offered a higher return than highly rated bonds. Even when the inevitable defaults were taken into account. This is the holy grail of investing. Finding mispriced assets. The low-grade — or junk — bonds were not priced appropriately given their risk.

The seeds of a revolution in finance were sown in that simple truth. You always need a simple truth for everything that will come. A north star for when people start thinking that what's happening doesn't make any sense. The notion that a diversified portfolio of junk bonds was safe was foundational to what happened next.

When Milken started his first job on Wall Street, he manoeuvred his way into a position to take advantage of this truth. There was one problem. The supply of junk bonds was limited. The only junk bonds were so-called *fallen angels*. This bit of finance jargon refers to formerly credit-grade bonds that have hit hard times.

While Milken showed some early profits in his foray into junk bonds, he wanted more. He had proved Hickman's thesis in a limited way and created some nascent demand for junk bonds. What he didn't have was enough supply. He needed newly issued junk bonds. Long story short, he finally got more supply by joining with an emerging force on Wall Street — the corporate raiders who were starting the first leveraged buyouts (LBOs).

These operators were taking companies private by loading them up with debt. They would restructure them and sell off parts or the whole of a company for a profit. Think Gordon Gekko in *Wall Street*, with his 'greed is good' line, admonishing management of the arrival of a new era in investing.

(continued)

The only way to issue the amount of debt needed to take a company private was to issue junk bonds. The companies were in too much debt to receive a strong credit rating. And Milken and his firm, Drexel Burnham Lambert, were the biggest players in this space. Whole deals were done on the basis of Milken issuing a 'highly confident' letter advising that he was confident he could find buyers for the junk bonds. Billion-dollar takeovers were consummated on his word.

The merging of junk bonds and leveraged buyouts was important. For investors in junk bonds, what was required was a unifying vision people could latch onto — the notion that Milken and the corporate raiders, and by extension LBOs and junk bonds, were good for America.

The story was simple. The country had grown complacent and lazy during the seventies, and Japan and West Germany were pulling ahead. LBOs would cut the fat and make America competitive again. This message conveniently had parallels with Reagan's political message. It explains why Gekko ended his 'greed is good' speech with the admonishment that greed will save 'that other malfunctioning corporation called the USA'.

Milken was the king of Wall Street. He moved his operation to LA to keep his meddlesome bosses in New York at bay and got himself a new toupee to fit his image. In the 1980s he was earning $107k an hour. The challenges Milken faced extended beyond his uncooperative follicles. He needed to match supply and demand for junk bonds. Each seller he found would need a buyer. And to keep demand up, he needed to make sure the principles first outlined in Hickman's page-turning bond thesis held true. Returns had to be strong.

Milken needed to keep the party going. There was a simple way to do this. The only way a junk-bond issuer could default was if they ran out of money. If the original junk bonds were rolled over continuously into new junk bonds, there would be no default. Milken just had to find new buyers. As time passed and the pile of junk bonds got bigger and bigger, this became harder. Soon he had to start making fraudulent claims, and these became bolder and bolder.

Eventually a young lawyer looking to make a name for himself as a precursor to a political career started sniffing around. Rudolph Giuliani began his Wall Street assault by prosecuting low-level players. Eventually the trail led to Milken, who was indicted on 98 counts of racketeering and fraud. He has the dubious distinction of being the first individual who wasn't in 'organised crime' to be indicted for organised crime.

Milken went to jail; Drexel Burnham Lambert imploded and filed for bankruptcy. Giuliani became New York's mayor. And the corporate raiders and LBOs? They rebranded. The three-piece suits and in-your-face eighties-style excess were traded for Patagonia vests, khakis and a projected image of benevolent capitalism. The industry's reincarnation was completed with a name change. Private equity seemed to fit the bill.

The investors who purchased the junk bonds suffered huge losses. Many of them were banking entities known as savings and loan associations ('S&Ls'). Hundreds of S&Ls eventually collapsed. The US government spent billions bailing them out but couldn't stave off a resulting major recession.

The overarching lesson is simple. Be mindful of runaway growth. Be alarmed when the foundation of that growth is a simple, widely recognised truth that gets combined with a unifying vision that the growth contributes positively to society.

Mark's early lesson in hype

I first started investing during the late 1990s during the dotcom bubble in the US. The optimism was off the charts. The emerging technology of the internet was early in its adoption cycle and the prevailing narrative was the new technology would reshape the world. The internet would change everything. It would make us more productive and change the way we buy and sell goods and services as well as the way we interact with the world and our fellow humans.

This vision was largely realised. Between 2000 and 2020 the number of internet users grew from 150 million to 4.5 billion. Today it plays such a large role in our lives that there is a movement to limit its use. On the surface this should have been an amazing investment.

Infrastructure was needed to support the internet's expansion, yet infrastructure investments performed terribly. Global Crossing and Worldcom, which laid the fibre to connect the world, went out of business. Shares in Cisco, which provided the networking equipment, was trading at such a high valuation that the share price is still below the high from 25 years ago. Microsoft took close to 15 years to reach a new high after the bubble burst.

The companies that provided access to the internet through search engines have all been crushed by Google, which didn't go public until 2004. Almost every early internet retailer went out of business and Amazon emerged from the wreckage.

The transformative vision of the technology did come to fruition. The internet was all it was cracked up to be. The implications from an investment perspective were less clear. Yet that didn't stop optimistic investors from crafting a narrative justification for such high valuations and a limitless future. I was one of those investors.

This early experience taught me that a compelling narrative does not necessarily make for a good investment. I learned that every narrative needs a universal truth to justify all sorts of fantastical outcomes. The snake-oil salesmen promoting a particular narrative can point to that truth to bludgeon any naysayers. As I've studied market history it has become clear to me that the same cycle repeats over and over again. This has made me deeply sceptical of hype and the impact it has on investors.

4. Overconfidence

Good investors are supposed to be confident investors. We accept that as a good thing and don't spend a lot of time thinking about the source of that confidence or the ramifications. Is it based on more knowledge and skill — or is it bluster? Does confidence help investors or hold them back?

Overtrading is a manifestation of overconfidence. Overconfidence bias describes investors who have an inflated sense of control and unrealistic optimism. This results in an underestimation of risk. It turns out that the human mind is really good at ego stroking. If an investor hears about another investor making a mistake, the poor outcome is often attributed to that investor's failings. But if we make the same mistake it is often attributed to a factor beyond our control. This is a perfect formula for not learning from mistakes — our own and those of others.

We convince ourselves that each new idea can't miss, that we can be nimble and constantly adjust our portfolio to take advantage of whatever is occurring in the short-term market environment.

Overconfidence also has an impact on portfolio construction. According to a Fidelity study, overconfident investors overload their portfolio with the riskiest assets. And while a case can be made that the short-term volatility associated with riskier assets matters little over the long term, it turns out that overconfident investors don't tend to hold them for the long term.

To prevent overtrading, focus on the three attributes that successful investors share — humility, consistency and patience. We will outline how you can build structure into your investing approach to help prevent overtrading. For now, we are off to a good start by identifying what is holding investors back from achieving financial freedom.

Shani's lesson on following the investment herd

All investors make mistakes. I've made plenty, and they have helped me understand the type of investor I am and what works best for me. But like a lot of investors who have entered the market in the past 15 years, I haven't experienced any sort of prolonged bear market to test my nerve.

This can lead to a false sense of security. You can feel you have the Midas touch. Issues arise when things start to go wrong, as they will. Bear markets occur every 3.5 years on average, so all long-term investors will experience them. The period I've experienced with sustained market growth is not the norm.

My false sense of security has led me to make some investments that were not aligned with what I want to achieve. Luckily for me I've mostly come out unscathed, but in one particular case my luck ran out.

Cathie Wood is the CEO of Ark Invest. In 2020 her ARK Innovation ETF gained 152.82 per cent. The year before, it achieved a 35.58 per cent return. In 2018 the ETF beat the average return of similar funds by over 10 per cent on the year before, and it returned 87.34 per cent the year before that. Many who saw these returns thought Cathie was a visionary.

I wanted to jump on this train, partly because of the eye-watering returns and partly because I was excited about a woman absolutely smoking the rest of the industry. Neither is a legitimate reason to invest and neither connected to my financial goals. Yet still I invested. ARK Innovation ETF is an active ETF that invests in 'disruptive innovation'. The thesis did not resonate with me. It was expensive. There was no reason for me to tilt towards innovation in my portfolio. I just wanted the returns.

I got burned and lost 40 per cent of my money, and I lost it at a time when I still had decades of compounding ahead of me.

You will face challenging periods as an investor, just as in life. Nobody would wish those periods on anyone, but the only way to make them positive is to make sure you learn from them and do better next time.

Psychologically a loss elicits more pain than the joy elicited from a gain. In some cases, investors retreat into the safety of a savings account after a loss. Why would I put my hand back on the stove that burned me? The truth is that the return on cash is not enough to enable me to reach my financial goals. In some cases, investors simply pretend the loss didn't happen, so they never learn the lesson and will make the same mistake again.

The simple solution is not to treat investing as a speculator's sport, even if that is easier said than done. Poor outcomes from individual investments, and years of bear markets, are inevitable. Make sure these experiences make you a better investor.

Keep the focus on your goals, and select investments that resonate with you. Accept that emotions are always at play when it comes to investing. Each investment ultimately satisfies an emotional desire — whether that is a comfortable retirement, a holiday or your children's education.

Exercise: Reduce future mistakes

We will provide you with a lot of data from studies illuminating the impact of poor behaviour and reinforcing what good investing habits look like. It's not about preaching, because no-one deliberately does things that harm future outcomes.

This exercise may be a little confronting for some people, but it is important to be a bit introspective about your investing behaviour. Investors tend to ignore or de-emphasise losses and focus on wins. This kind of behaviour is common to all aspects of life. The issue is that without a realistic view of how things are going, it is hard to change. Open up your brokerage statements and try to work out the following:

- How many times do you trade in a typical year? By 'trade' we mean selling one investment and buying another. Exclude any buy transactions on new contributions into your account.
- In each one of your trades, how long was your holding period for the investments you sold? Categorise them and place them in less-than-one-year and more-than-one-year buckets.

- Try to provide the rationale for each investment. Go beyond 'hoping it would go up in price' to consider why you thought the price would increase. Ideally you will also be able to offer a rationale for why you thought this particular investment was right for you.

This exercise should enable you to recognise areas to focus on. Generally, the more an investor trades, the lower their returns. Holding periods of less than a year have worse tax outcomes than holding periods of more than a year. Buying investments without a clear rationale makes it less likely that you will hold them through the inevitable ups and downs of the market. That leads to trading more, which starts the whole cycle again.

Knowing more about your own behaviour gives you a baseline as you start to build structure around your investing approach. This will inform the personalised plan we will help you put together in the remainder of the book.

Key takeaways

One of the biggest drivers of returns is your own behaviour. Your actions are completely within your control, yet many investors sabotage their outcomes. Common items that trip up investors include falling for hype, being overconfident, following advice designed for investors with different goals and confusing complexity for competence.

Introspection is an important step in figuring out what you are already doing right and where you can improve. That was the point of the exercise in the previous chapter examining your money philosophy and the influences on how you think about money. Critically examining your own investing behaviour is an important step in defining a personalised plan that will enable you to achieve financial independence. Examining your own investing behaviour will enable you to put the right structure in place to support your investment strategy and prevent the mistakes that derail investors.

A clear path to follow

There's a story that Vanguard founder John Bogle really liked about an exchange between two acclaimed American novelists. He liked it so much he named one of his books after it. Kurt Vonnegut took his good friend Joseph Heller to a party at a house on Shelter Island, a wealthy community off the coast of Long Island, New York. Vonnegut teasingly informed Heller that the billionaire hedge-fund manager hosting the party made more money in a single day than Heller's total earnings on *Catch-22*, his most popular and financially successful work.

Refusing to take the bait, Heller responded, 'Yes, but I have something he will never have — enough!'

Enough is the title Bogle chose for his book on the destructive impact of society's obsession with the pursuit of wealth. We will focus on the impact of that obsession on your investment account.

Vonnegut and Heller's conversation comes to mind every time an investor tells us their goal is to accumulate the most money possible. It's the number one objection we hear when we talk about goals-based investing. Many investors don't think they need to come up with goals because their goal is surely self-evident — to have more. We don't believe having a defined goal will hold you back from building wealth. We think people sabotage their future by never having enough.

How not to accomplish your financial goals

We will return to the inversion technique because, unsurprisingly, what we'll propose is ignored by most investors. They don't see the point. We disagree, so in the spirit of inversion, here are the best ways to ensure you will never reach financial independence.

Step one is not having a goal. Building wealth requires sacrificing current spending for saving. Without a goal you are far less likely to continue to sacrifice things you want now for a future you haven't bothered to define. Building wealth requires patience, foresight and consistency over decades. As long as you don't have a goal, you won't have a reliable guide to making the best financial decisions.

Another way to not achieve financial independence is to imagine you do have a goal but to define it so vaguely that it not only provides no benefit but actually hampers your efforts to get ahead. We are referring to people whose vague goals are 'getting rich' or 'having the most money possible'.

What is tempting about this goal is that it seems logical. Who wouldn't want to have the most money possible? To understand why a nebulously defined goal is unhelpful requires an examination of the purpose of a goal. Goals not only help you form a plan; they continue to guide decision making and provide motivation. They are part of the framework that helps you tune out noise, dampen emotions and focus on the long term.

A vague goal of having the most money possible does none of those things. Any decision or action you take can be justified. It allows even the most well-motivated investor to indulge in any and every emotional impulse. It is a formula for timing the market, trading frequently and chasing performance. All of these actions make sense since having the most money possible means an investor should always be in the 'best' investments. As we've discussed, that is a sure-fire way never to become financially independent.

Failing to define a goal or defining it vaguely prevents you from creating a financial plan. If you happen to reach financial independence it will be the result of dumb luck. You don't know how much to save. You don't know what return you need to achieve your desired outcome. You can't make an informed decision on asset allocation or how much risk you take.

To sum up, if you want to guarantee never achieving financial independence, there are few things more effective than failing to come up with a well-defined goal.

Does this sound like the way you handle your finances? Are you aimlessly taking actions you think will make a difference with no actual idea of how they will impact your future? The good news is that coming up with a well-defined goal is not difficult. In this chapter we explain why goals are so important and the steps to take to define them.

Why do we believe in goals-based investing? The simple answer is that you can't figure out how to get somewhere without knowing where you are going. The more complex answer requires an exploration of the two secrets to achieving financial independence.

Mark says...

To summarise, investing is hard. The more you immerse yourself in the investing world, the harder it seems. Everyone has a different opinion on what to do and how to do it. It can make your head spin to try and make sense of it all. Yet none of these people know what I'm trying to accomplish. Knowing my goals allows me to sift through the noise and focus on taking a consistent approach with my decision making. Gaining financial independence isn't about being the smartest or most knowledgeable person. It is about having a plan and following it over decades. That all starts with goals.

Follow an approach perfectly tailored for you

To reiterate, to be successful requires an investment strategy that is designed to meet your unique goals and takes into account your temperament and intellectual outlook. We hear passionate advocacy for specific investment approaches all the time, but it's important to remain aware that many advocates benefit financially from investors taking their advice.

We are agnostic when it comes to investment approaches. We don't think there is one right way to invest, but we do think there is a right way for you to invest based on your circumstances and goals. Later we will outline our own approaches, which are very different though based on the same foundational concepts. As we've explained, our goal is to enable you to find the approach that's right for you.

Many investors think the key to success is action, but the only way for you to find the investment approach that's right for you is to spend time thinking about what you are trying to achieve. Often the best thing you can do in the short term is nothing. A goal and a strategy to achieve that goal provides an anchor to keep you focused on the long term so you are able to filter out ideas that don't align with your strategy.

This process of filtering can improve decision making. As psychologist Daniel Kahneman has advised, 'Wherever you look at human judgments, you are likely to find noise. To improve the quality of our judgments, we need to overcome noise as well as bias.' One way to eliminate noise is to eliminate options from consideration. We will address this point in chapter 9.

Success in any endeavour is a function of finding your competitive advantage and making that the focus of your actions. No-one knows more about you and what you want out of life than you do. Not the most brilliant hedge fund manager. Not the professional investor with every degree under the sun and decades of experience. You are the foremost expert on you and the only one who can come up with the perfect approach to achieve your goals.

Minimising mistakes

You will make mistakes. We've both made them. Every investor does. But while acknowledging this, we can still work to minimise them and their impact on results. Investing is an intellectual exercise. The outcome you achieve will be the result of countless decisions made over decades. A well-defined goal and investment strategy provides both a framework and a structure for your decision making. Structure ensures consistency. Consistency leads to success. It is a simple concept but one that can be difficult to execute.

The goal of having the most money possible lacks structure. As we outlined in our inversion exercise, the logical pathway to this goal is always to be constantly chasing the 'best' performance. You are more susceptible to the compelling narrative that often accompanies a speculative investment. It leads you to trade too much, which leads you to pay more in taxes and transaction fees. There's nothing holding you back from making a series of poor decisions.

The evidence that this directionless approach is the pathway to poor investment outcomes is overwhelming. Let's review the significant impact of poor behaviour.

Odean and Barber's research, you'll recall, showed that investments purchased underperformed those sold by an average of 3.32 per cent after 504 trading days. And the returns of those who traded least were over 30 per cent higher than the returns of those who traded most. The Morningstar 'Mind the Gap' report showed the impact of poor timing decisions meant that investors underperformed the investments they bought and sold by up to 1.60 per cent a year. Such poor behaviour shows why most people don't achieve financial freedom.

What holds investors back is the pervasive poor behaviour of trading too much. You'll recollect that in June 2020 the average holding period of a share trading on the New York Stock Exchange was five and a half months, down from 14 months in 2019. The average holding period has been dropping for decades from a high of eight years in the mid 1960s.

Professional investors are not immune to this behaviour. According to Michael Laske, a former Morningstar researcher, the average turnover ratio for US domestic equity funds was 63 per cent in 2019. That means that every year more than half of the positions were new.

All this frenetic activity means investors are squandering the largesse of the wealth-generating engine that is the financial markets.

There's no single reason why investors are trading more, but undoubtedly the removal of friction to trade plays a role. Executing a trade used to involve a call to a broker. At the very least this would give your broker the opportunity to talk you out of doing something against your best interests. Today we can trade with a couple clicks on our phones without any human interaction.

Many investors who know better still exhibit this behaviour. There's a powerful psychological impact associated with anonymity. We navigate between two different versions of ourselves. The public version is the one the world sees, the persona that adheres to societal norms. For knowledgeable investors, the public persona is often committed to the Buffett maxim that the best holding period is forever. Then there's our private self whose behaviours we keep hidden, because we know they are not always in our best interest so reflect poorly on us. Your private self absent-mindedly trades on your phone on the way to lunch.

Poor decisions lead to poor outcomes. We believe most investors make too many poor decisions to achieve the results they need to accomplish their goals. Most investors also don't bother to spend time establishing goals and thinking through the implications of those goals on how they invest and what they invest in. We think the two are closely linked.

It is said, probably incorrectly, that Einstein first defined insanity as doing the same thing over and over and expecting different results. To succeed as an investor, you will embark on a journey that's different from those taken by most investors. You will start that journey by going through the goal definition process.

Set a goal because it works

The best reason for doing anything is the simplest one — because it works. Research into goal-setting theory by US psychologists Edwin Locke and Gary Latham shows that people are more committed to goals that are personalised, important to them, well-specified and accurately measured. This strengthens the case for ensuring your financial goals are at the centre of your investment strategy, because they will help to combat poor behaviour.

When it comes to investment success, vague, nonquantitative goals such as 'do your best' resulted in subpar results in 51 out of 53 studies (96 per cent of the time). On the other hand, 'significant' or 'contingently significant effects' are the result of clear, specific goals.

David Blanchett, Morningstar's Head of Retirement Research, has shown that centring your portfolio on financial goals can increase portfolio values for investors by 15 per cent over the lifetime of their goals. Ryan Murphy and Samantha Lamas, also of Morningstar, conducted research in 2018 showing that the benefits of goals go beyond returns. Goal setting results in investors feeling motivated and satisfied. So there is a strong case for goals as the basis of your portfolio.

Shani says ...

I understand the importance of having defined goals as an investor, because when I started out I didn't have any. I used to be one of those investors who focused more on investments than investing. I purchased funds that had sex appeal, with terms like 'pure alpha', 'long–short' or 'innovation' in the name. I was extremely lucky that I invested during a very long bull run.

Things are different now. My portfolio is connected to a solid foundation — my goals. I have a strong understanding of why I hold each position and why it behaves the way it does through different market conditions. This understanding and the connection to my goals mean that I am not tempted by each new opportunity. I have a long time horizon for my capital to grow and compound. I've evolved my perception of investing from maximising wealth to building a model that works best to maximise my outcomes.

Define your investment goal

Spending time thinking about the destination you want to reach will give you an opportunity to figure out the best way to get there. We will iteratively build on why and how to do that in subsequent chapters. For now we'll walk you through the process of properly defining a goal.

The first step is to think about how your financial assets can enable you to live the life you want. We'll get into the numbers, but for now focus on your dreams. Investing is simply a means to an end. It's likely you already have a foundation based on your money philosophy.

Morningstar has researched ways to optimise the goal-setting process. Although the research focuses on how financial advisers can help their clients during this process, it is just as useful for self-directed investors.

We need to overcome our cognitive biases. In some ways we are all strangers to ourselves, and what you see as a financial goal might not reflect your true motivation.

The investors who participated in the Morningstar study were asked outright to name their financial goals (figure 5.1). They tended to list common financial goals — for example, retirement or buying a house.

These are called 'surface goals'. When investors instead applied a framework to dig deeper into what it was they really wanted, such as donating to causes they believed in and maintaining relationships with family and friends, their goals changed to reflect their values. These are called 'deeper goals'. This is similar to the process we encouraged you to go through to define your financial philosophy.

A surface goal might be the purchase of a holiday house. Further reflection might lead to the goal being changed to, say, spending more quality time with the family. Defining a goal at a deeper level may reveal more options for recognising and achieving what you truly want.

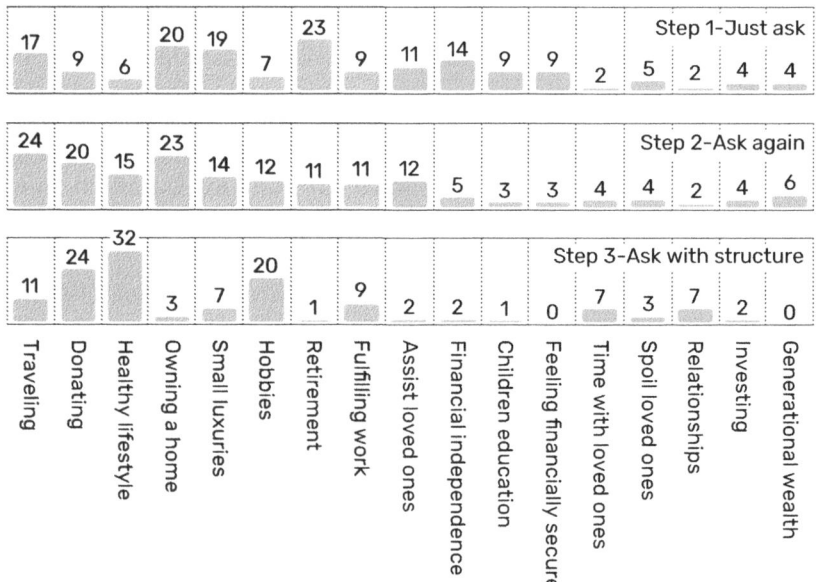

Figure 5.1: percentage of people mentioning goals at each stage
Source: Morningstar research

The results of the study showed that treating your goal setting as a multi-step process can help you better understand what you want and what will make you happy.

Exercise: Define deeper goals

It's time to take out your notebook again and start to define your goals. If you have a partner, do this exercise separately then compare notes. Take your time and really think it through.

The aim is to come up with better goals. In the Morningstar study, 75 per cent of people changed at least one of their top three financial goals after going through this process.

Step 1: List your top three financial goals. (Don't feel tied to what first comes to mind or embarrassed if you change your mind later.)

- Most important goal
- Second-most important goal
- Third-most important goal

Step 2: Take a look at the following list of common financial goals. Are any of the goals on the list important to you? Write down the ones that are.

- To be better off than my peers
- To pay for personal self-improvement (for example, to go back to school or to learn a skill)
- To experience the excitement of investing
- To start a new business
- To buy a house
- To help pay for my kids' university education
- To stop working and do something I love
- To go on a dream holiday

(continued)

- To relocate in retirement
- To care for my ageing parents
- To give to a charity or other causes I care about
- To feel secure about my finances in retirement
- To feel secure about my finances now
- To leave an inheritance to my loved ones
- To retire early
- To pay for future medical expenses
- To avoid being a financial burden to my family as I grow older
- To manage my debt

Step 3: Write down your top three goals, in order of importance, from the master list.

- Most important goal
- Second-most important goal
- Third-most important goal

Step 4 (optional): Revisit the master list of common financial goals and cross out the goals that are least important to you. Sometimes identifying what you don't care about can help clarify what really drives you.

Transform your goals into the basis of a plan

Now you have a list of goals, it's time to define them in order to inform the approach you take with your finances. The following information is needed:

- How much do you currently have saved for your goal?
- How many years until you want to achieve your goal?

- How much money will you need to accomplish your goal?
- How much can you save annually towards your goal?

We will provide pointers for each of these steps during the next goal-setting exercise. We outline our own personal examples later in this chapter. First, some theory to get you started.

We know that many investors will find this exercise difficult if the goal is far out in the future. Circumstances change and our goals change over time. That's okay. It's far easier to adjust a baseline than to be completely in the dark about what it will take to accomplish your goal.

Going through this process will allow you to make more informed choices as you're confronted with life decisions. Should you take a lower-paying job? What are the implications of taking time away from work? What should you do with a windfall or a raise? Contextualising the impact on your finances will help you make good decisions.

The purpose of defining a goal in this way is that each step is an input needed to calculate the return needed to achieve your goal. This is a concept known as the time value of money (TVM) and it shows how changing each of the variables in the formula impacts how much money you will end up with in the future.

This should make sense intuitively. If you have more money saved, you'll have more in the future. If you save more money, you'll have more in the future. If your investments earn a higher return, you'll have more money in the future. The formula takes that intuition and shows the actual impact of changing each variable. This can help inform the decisions you make.

We can demonstrate this using a hypothetical example of a $1 million retirement goal. If you have $50 000 saved and want to retire in 20 years, and you plan to save $5000 a year, you can calculate the return needed to achieve your desired outcome. In this example, an annual return of 13.10 per cent is needed. Calculating the return needed is a good way of assessing whether the goal is feasible. In this case, the goal is unrealistic for most investors. Time to go back to the drawing board.

Table 5.1 represents 30-year returns on different asset classes over the past 30 years.

As you can see, an annual return of 13.10 per cent far exceeds the highest long-term historic return of any asset class. These returns also do not include any fees an investor might pay or the impact of taxes. We recommend that most investors aim for a goal that does not require a return higher than 7 to 8 per cent. We go into more detail when we address asset allocation, but for now let's go back and try to adjust the goal.

One option is to save more money, which will lower the return needed. Saving $17500 a year will lower the required return to 7.70 per cent, for example. Much better. Another option is to retire later. Delaying retirement by 10 years also lowers the return to 7.70 per cent. The last option is to lower the goal. If you lower the retirement goal from $1000000 to $445000, the required return is once again 7.70 per cent a year.

Table 5.1: annual returns by asset class

Asset class	Nominal annual return over 30 years (%)
US shares	11.10
Australian shares	9.10
International shares	8.20
Australian listed property	7.80
Australian bonds	5.60
Cash	4.20

Source: Morningstar data

This hypothetical example demonstrates how the goal-setting process allows you to see the feasibility of a goal and make financial decisions that will ensure you reach it. Life is about trade-offs and using this approach to goal setting makes their impact transparent.

Most people are on cruise control for a goal like retirement and don't bother to figure out how things are going until it's imminent. As we pointed out earlier, course correcting is extremely hard late in life.

Exercise: Define your detailed goal

Time to try this yourself. Pick a goal and come up with an estimate for each of these inputs. Remember that a ballpark figure is all you need.

Step 1: How much do you currently have saved for your goal?

This is potentially the most straightforward input. Time to get your account statements out to see where you stand.

Step 2: How many years until you want to achieve your goal?

This is also a relatively straightforward component of the inputs. Yet many investors may want to include a range and model out the differences. Perhaps you want to see what it would take to retire in 20 or 25 years. Play around with the variables.

(continued)

Step 3: How much money do you need to accomplish your goal?

Depending on the goal, this can be an easy or a hard step. Retirement is challenging, and we've dedicated a special section to estimating how much you will need in retirement later in this chapter.

One key requirement is to take inflation into account. We recommend calculating how much your goal would cost today then applying a projected inflation percentage to estimate what it will cost in the future. Over the long term a 2 to 3 per cent annual increase in prices is appropriate, with 3 per cent being more conservative.

For now, assess in today's dollars and come up with an inflation estimate. In the calculation section we will outline how to incorporate inflation into your estimate.

If you want an accurate assessment for a goal that involves supporting yourself, we suggest you use a personal inflation rate as an input into your goal-planning process. Official inflation rates are based on 'an ordinary household'. Your spending patterns may differ greatly from such a household. They may differ even more when you realise your goal. It is also influenced by where you live, which may be more or less expensive than the average.

A personal inflation rate is a benchmark for maintaining purchasing power. The good news is that understanding your personal inflation rate is a guide to your investment strategy. Table 5.2 shows the weighting of each budgetary category based on an ordinary basket of goods.

Table 5.2: CPI expenditure weighting for 2024

Group	Weighting in 2024 (%)
Food and non-alcoholic beverages	17.15
Alcohol and tobacco	6.98
Clothing and footwear	3.40
Housing	21.74
Furnishings, household equipment and services	8.43
Health	6.43
Transport	11.42
Communication	2.14
Recreation and culture	12.55
Education	4.34
Insurance and financial services	5.43

Source: Australian Bureau of Statistics 2024, Annual weight update of the CPI and Living Cost Indexes, https://www.abs.gov.au/articles/annual-weight-update-cpi-and-living-cost-indexes, accessed 3 July 2025.

When we went through this exercise we found that our costs varied significantly from those of the ordinary basket of goods. Neither of us owns a vehicle and we live centrally and walk to most places. We don't have personal education costs. Shani's housing expenses are higher than the basket, as she has a mortgage on an inner-city home. You can see how your expenses would alter the inflation rate you would use and might look markedly different from the 2 to 3 per cent average.

To calculate your personal inflation rate, you need to understand your expenses and fit them into the appropriate baskets. Each basket will have a different inflation rate, which you can source from the ABS. The inflation rate changes quarterly, but it is not necessary to recalculate this every quarter for long-term goals.

For investors who are using the inflation rate as an input to calculate long-term goals, again it is worth considering the drivers of a drastic change in your personal inflation rate, such as one-off expenses or abnormal economic environments that will not continue over a longer period. Over time inflation tends to fall within a 2 to 3 per cent band in Australia, and your personal inflation rate will likely behave similarly so you will be able to use the Australian inflation rate as a guide. It is unlikely that you will experience large rises or falls often, but stay informed about whether it is worth moving the goalposts.

Step 4: How much can you save annually towards your goal?

This is a fourth step that requires some effort depending on your personal situation. Be honest with yourself and understand how much you can save sustainably. To this end we recommend taking a yearly look at your income and your expenditure. This will capture all the annual, one-off expenses like car registration or home insurance. We're talking about what is commonly known as a budget. There are great, free tools available, such as the Budget Planner on Moneysmart.

If you are early in your career, a salary increase may be an opportunity to save more money. At other times you are not able to save as much. Your expenses may increase if your circumstances change — for example, if you start a family.

One approach is to come up with different phases in your life with different savings rates. Another is to come up with a minimal savings rate and see where you land and then adopt a more aggressive savings level for the top range of potential outcomes. The most important thing to understand is that saving early in life is significantly better than saving late in life. That is one of the lessons learned from our exploration of compounding.

What if you don't have a goal?

Psychologist and Harvard professor Daniel Gilbert articulated a phenomenon he termed the end-of-history illusion. The concept is that at almost any age, people generally acknowledge they've changed a great deal in the past — but they resist the idea that they will change much in the future. The fact is, of course, that we all continue to change throughout our lives. Our interests change, our friends change, our motivations change and our values change. We tend to underestimate either the constancy or the magnitude of such changes.

We hear a lot about how we need to build financial security to prepare for the inevitable challenges of life — job losses, health problems and unexpected expenses. We couldn't agree more, yet life is about more than trying to stave off disaster. A life worth living is also about pursuing our passions and interests.

One point we make repeatedly is that financial freedom is synonymous with choice. We invest because we want to be able to have choices in our lives. We may not know what we will want in the future, but that doesn't mean we shouldn't strive for the financial flexibility that permits us to pursue whatever may come up.

It can be hard to equate a goal with financial freedom. A goal is tangible and finite. Financial freedom is not so straightforward. This chapter's focus is on why it is important to set a goal. A goal provides structure to our decision making as well as motivation. The process of defining a goal facilitates the creation of a plan to achieve it.

There are plenty of goals that may not mean anything in an absolute sense but that contribute positively to our lives. For instance, many people come up with arbitrary fitness goals such as being able to run 10 kilometres by a certain date. The goal isn't really about running 10 kilometres — the distance in itself is meaningless and won't be of any practical use in anyone's life. The real goal is improved fitness through exercise, which is likely to have positive impacts. Since 'fitness' and 'exercise' are indeterminate concepts, we set a concrete goal (10 kilometres) in order to develop a plan and provide motivation. Investors, too, need concrete goals.

Come up with a savings goal and invest a certain amount of money regularly over the next years even if you don't know exactly what it's for. Not only will the money give you more options in the future, but you'll have instilled the habit of saving and investing. Go through the exercise to learn how much those savings could grow in the future. This knowledge will provide you with the motivation to keep going.

Exercise: Perform the calculations needed for your goal

You will need a financial calculator, a device that allows you to make the calculations typically used in business and investing, including interest, cash flow and amortisation calculations.

There are some subtle differences among financial calculators. For this book we used a calculator found at fncalculator.com. Click on 'TVM Calculator' in the upper left-hand corner of the webpage. You'll recall that TVM stands for time value of money.

We use terms that may confuse some readers, so here are some tips:

- The mode section allows a user to select the beginning or the end of the period. In the case of a monthly payment, this would indicate the investment occurs at the beginning or the end of the month.

- It's important to match the frequency of the payments with the number of periods involved. If the contribution is monthly and you are measuring the time until your goal in years, you need to convert the time to months – 360 months would indicate 30 years. Alternatively, you could multiply your monthly savings by 12. This will make a small difference in the calculation, but either option works; the point is to produce a ballpark estimate.

- The future value (FV) figure is negative, which may confuse some readers. This is a quirk of financial calculators. Technically any cash flow invested is a negative cash flow, as you are taking cash and putting it into an investment. The current investment and each of the contributions should have been negative numbers, which would make the future value positive. In practical terms this is irrelevant so long as you bear in mind that the negative value should be thought of as a positive number.

- The calculator allows a user to select the compounding period. Compounding is earning a return on a return. The more frequent the compounding, the higher the final total amount. Generally, we calculate sharemarket returns on an annual basis, so we suggest you select the most conservative option, which is annual.

(continued)

Based on your estimates for each component of the TVM formula, enter the data provided in table 5.3 into the calculator.

Table 5.3: calculator fields and how they tie to your goals

TVM calculator field	Step in goal definition
Present value	How much do you currently have saved for your goal?
Payments	How much can you save for your goal (match to the time until goal achieved)?
Future value	This is how much you need for your goal in future dollars (see inflation calculation below).
Annual rate (%)	This is what you are calculating, so leave it blank.
Periods	This is the time within which you want to achieve your goal (match to the savings amount frequency).

How to incorporate inflation

Prices change over time. In this case we are assuming an annual increase in the cost of achieving your goal and including that in our calculations. Use the same financial calculator and the data in table 5.4 to incorporate inflation into your estimate of how much achieving your goal will cost in the future.

This calculation is the number you should use as the cost of your goal when you calculate the required rate of return.

Table 5.4: calculator fields and how they relate to your goals, incorporating inflation

TVM calculator field	Step in goal definition
Present value	How much does your goal cost in today's dollars?
Payments	Enter '0' into this field.
Future value	This is what you are calculating, so leave it blank.
Annual rate (%)	This is your annual estimate of inflation.
Periods	This is the time within which you want to achieve your goal. If you are using an annual inflation estimate, use years until your goal.

How to estimate your retirement needs

Retirement planning presents a particular challenge as many investors struggle to figure out a dollar amount at retirement that will generate a sustainable annual withdrawal to pay for living expenses.

This step-by-step process can be used by investors of any age to estimate the size of their retirement portfolio. Over the course of your working life you will have been conditioned to think of day-to-day spending in terms of a set salary. And this is a good place to start with retirement planning. In retirement your 'salary' will come from your portfolio rather than from an employer.

A good starting point is to use your current salary to determine what you need to replicate your current standard of living. This is especially pertinent for people approaching retirement but also works for younger investors as you can adjust your current standard of living into the future.

Step 1: Tax and savings adjustments

There are two initial adjustments you can make to your salary when trying to determine what it will cost to maintain your standard of living in retirement. The first is the taxes you pay. Most investors who access superannuation to pay for retirement can eliminate taxes. In the pension phase of superannuation withdrawals will not be taxed if you meet the age requirements. Look at a pay slip and remove the amount you presently pay in taxes.

The next adjustment is to remove the amount of your salary you are saving. At the very least you can remove the compulsory super contribution. For some investors, the savings rate will be higher given additional contributions to super or savings outside of super.

Step 2: Lifestyle adjustments

The next set of adjustments is for lifestyle changes in retirement. This requires some thought about your retirement plans. If you are moving to a cheaper location to retire, now is the opportunity to adjust your spending needs downward.

If you anticipate major changes in retirement, such as having paid off your house, you can remove mortgage repayments from your spending needs.

Think about other ways in which your spending needs may shift in retirement. Many retirees initially spend more money. The freedom of not being tied down by a job may mean more travel or higher day-to-day spending given the additional time for activities.

If you are years from retirement you might decide to skip this step as it will include so many unknowns.

Step 3: Taking salary inflation into account

This step can be skipped if you are close to retirement. Investors with a longer time horizon will need to make adjustments for cost-of-living increases and the lifestyle creep that generally occurs as we age.

Estimate the salary increase percentage you expect annually until your retirement. Use the same steps to calculate your salary at retirement as the inflation adjustment. Remove the same percentages as savings and taxes represent in relation to your current salary. Your marginal tax rate may change over time and tax rates and brackets will also likely change. This is only a ballpark estimate, so don't get bogged down in the details.

Step 4: Adjust for other sources of income

The final step is to make adjustments for other sources of income during retirement. Your goal is to come up with an annual spending total that can be supported by your portfolio. Sources of income that will not come from your portfolio need to be removed to estimate how much you will need.

One example of a non-portfolio income source is the age pension but there are other potential sources, including investment property, a private pension, an annuity or part-time employment if you are not fully retired.

Younger investors may choose to exclude this step from your estimate if you are not confident that a potential income source, such as the age pension, will exist in its current form when you retire.

Step 5: Convert annual spending needs to a lump sum

At this stage you should be able to estimate how much you'll need to spend annually in future dollars. Sense check what you came up with using the '70 per cent of your current salary' rule of thumb often used for retirement estimates.

Once you know your spending requirements, take the final step and calculate how large your portfolio will need to be. This is a simple calculation. Divide your spending needs by an annual withdrawal rate.

If your estimated retirement spending needs are $69 000 and your rate of withdrawal is 4 per cent, simply divide 69 000 by 0.04, which will give you a total portfolio size of $1 725 000.

The safe withdrawal rate is the amount you can take out of your portfolio from your first year of retirement with a reasonable chance your money will last your life. This safe withdrawal rate factors in changes to the amount you take out after your first year to adjust for inflation so you can maintain a consistent standard of living.

Traditionally the safe withdrawal rate is based on a 30-year retirement, which covers the possibility you may live a long time. If you envision retiring early, the withdrawal rate may have to be meaningfully reduced to allow for a longer retirement period.

A 4 per cent safe withdrawal rate is the personal finance benchmark and can be used if you are a long way off retirement. If you are nearing it, current retirement market conditions will dictate the returns you receive on your portfolio going forward.

We could write an entire book on withdrawal rates. If you are closer to retirement we would suggest you spend additional time researching withdrawal rates.

Shani's investing goals

The focus of this book is the pivotal role investing plays in attaining financial independence. It wasn't until I had completed my studies in finance and commerce at university and started my working life in a financial advice firm that I realised the importance of investing to building a comfortable life. Our clients largely fell into two buckets.

The focused

These clients had been thoughtful about investing over the long term. Although this didn't necessarily translate into large sums of money, this group understood what they could do with the resources they had and remained focused on their long-term outcomes.

When a financial adviser first 'onboards' a client, you ask them to fill out a few forms to help you understand more about them and what they want to achieve. This is called a Fact Find, which is similar to the process we outlined when we discussed goal setting earlier in this chapter.

An obvious marker of a focused client is how they complete this Fact Find. They will have a deep understanding of why they are investing, having defined their life goals and knowing what they want to achieve. They understand investments are a means to an end. They may not love the volatility of the market, but they understand why it is a necessary evil. Whether or not they can articulate it, they have accepted our view of risk. And they understand it is important to focus on

(continued)

---

the long term, so they have invested even when it has brought them some discomfort.

The way an adviser adds value for focused clients is by maximising their outcomes through structuring, tax minimisation and helping them finetune their investments so they will reach their goals.

The unfocused

Unfocused investors are motivated to create a better life for themselves but do not know how to do so. They don't have a proper understanding of their goals and what they are trying to achieve. Their Fact Find reflects what they think they want, but it is heavily influenced by social norms and societal expectations – in other words, the surface goals we addressed in the exercise earlier in this chapter.

Unfocused investors do not have a realistic picture of what is achievable given their resources and circumstances. In some cases they have vastly inflated expectations and in others they have no inkling of what is possible. In either case they cannot make a connection between their financial resources and their lives.

Advisers help unfocused clients adjust their expectations and help them to define their goals. They explain the important role investing plays in maximising their outcomes in order to achieve these goals. Again, this takes us back to our goal-setting exercise. The investor can see that if the required rate of return is too high, then expectations are unrealistic. If it is too low, the investor can dream bigger.

When I was just out of university and working for this financial advice firm I would have struggled to articulate the differences between focused and unfocused clients. Perhaps that is because I was in the unfocused bucket myself.

I was young and had an unrealistic view of both my career and financial potential. Despite working for a financial adviser, I didn't see investing as something for me. The clients that came in for financial advice were older than I was and typically had accumulated significant assets. Given the cost of financial advice and the increasing need for it as you get older, this wasn't surprising. I still couldn't see the pathway between where I was – with negative net assets and earning less than minimum wage – and where our clients were. My next job allowed me to negotiate that pathway.

Learning that investing is for me

Holistic financial advice, when applied correctly, touches every part of your finances. It covers taxes, investment structures, estate planning and picking investments. There's a lot to cover to ensure financial health. I realised very quickly that I had an affinity for one aspect of the process over the others. I couldn't get enough of investments and the mechanics of constructing portfolios. I'm not exactly sure why. Maybe because investing was such a foreign concept to me. Perhaps my lack of exposure growing up made it seem like I was being let in on a secret. Either way, I knew that investment advice was the aspect of the industry that interested me most.

I moved on to a job in asset management. Asset managers, or fund managers, invest the pooled funds of many investors. If you hold a managed fund or an ETF, the company that manages it is an asset manager. It was here that I resolved to get started with investing. I worked in client services looking at transaction histories and account balances all day. My job was to answer questions from clients and respond to requests about their investments.

I came to see account statements as a blueprint for building wealth. I'm naturally curious about other people's lives, and

(continued)

these statements were a snapshot of an aspect of people's lives that is generally hidden and that seemed so different from my own. I saw how people had built up their portfolios over time.

I had always thought investing was for rich people and had never spent much time pondering how people built their wealth, but now I had a front-row seat to how wealth was generated over time.

At this point I was 23 years old, earning $56 000 a year and living out of home in a very expensive city. Working in this role allowed me to see every scenario imaginable play out, one of which really hit home for me. Some people set aside only small weekly amounts over decades. This seemed achievable to me. I reasoned that to attain a comfortable life I needed to focus on saving to build up my capital base while I was young and could leverage the time I had. My first financial goal was to be able to build an emergency fund and not live pay cheque to pay cheque.

So I had a desire to invest, but no plan. I knew about managed funds because that was the only product this asset manager sold. Mark and I are always preaching about investing in what you know and understand. That's what I did, but having no point of comparison defeats the purpose. I still invest in managed funds, which are a core part of my investment portfolio. But more on that later.

I did what most investors do when they understand they need to invest. I focused on what to invest in rather than how to invest. I hadn't thought through my approach. I invested across a range of managed funds that had sexy names and great track records, because I wanted to get started as soon as possible. I had access to the portfolio models of the most successful financial advisers in Australia, and I just copied what they did. Surely I would succeed if I invested in funds that were chosen by financial advisers who had such carefully planned portfolios.

I would later discover that other than sexy names little differentiated these funds from one another. They were for all practical intents and purposes the same, with a lot of overlap in terms of the Australian equities in which they invested. They also all charged a premium management fee. I had no idea how these investments connected to any of my financial goals. Even worse, I didn't even know that investments should connect to your financial goals. In theory, they connected to the goals of the investor's portfolio I was copying.

I now know how foolhardy I was in copying the investment strategy of someone who was nothing like me, but I just wanted to maximise the wealth I had. Truth be told, I had no idea what my financial goals were. I was investing in 'the future' without having any sense of what it might look like or when I might reach it.

I was very lucky that for the time I was in those funds the markets prospered and I made a decent return. This won't always be the case, of course. Alongside the returns, I also learned a few lessons from these holdings. The first was about cash-flow management and the consequence of having successful investments. For someone who hasn't invested before and is on a modest salary, the bill from the ATO can be a shock. This was exacerbated for me by my student loans. The second lesson I learned concerned my behaviour: I realised I was comfortable with someone else choosing what individual shares to buy in these funds. I liked this model of outsourcing investment decisions.

It wasn't a perfect situation, but I had crossed an important threshold — I was an investor!

(continued)

How to get ahead in life

For much of my childhood I lived in a one-income household in which my father focused on paying down the mortgage and affording simple pleasures for his children. My parents had to contend with an expensive country with a young family while still having caring and financial responsibilities in Sri Lanka. I am very proud of the way both my parents navigated the new environment and the hard work and determination they both put in. Success for them lay in giving their daughters the opportunity to create comfortable lives in Australia. Our pathway seemed clear to them:

- Study hard.
- Get a good, stable job.
- Get married.
- Buy a house and pay down the mortgage.
- Build our savings.

I don't think this is different from what most parents hope for their children. They understood financial security to be the best path to a comfortable life. Truthfully, I have followed many of those steps to financial security. But they aren't a pathway to financial independence. What I didn't realise until I started working was that the opportunities I have been afforded allowed me to consider another aspect of money: it is an enabler to living the life you want.

This was not a sudden epiphany. Over time, as I gained confidence, I realised that investing wasn't just for other people — I could do this. I started to experience more career success. My portfolio was starting to grow and my savings rates increased. And I started to shake off my scarcity mindset and begin thinking about other possibilities.

Confidence can be a good and a bad thing for an investor. It can lead investors to take on more risk and to invest in things they don't fully understand. I was one of those investors early in my career.

But the good times kept rolling as equity markets continued to trounce other asset classes. I started off in managed funds but as my career progressed I felt an obligation to start making direct investments in shares. This is what people in the investment industry did.

I may not have been burned, but I was sitting in a stockpot that was slowly coming to a rolling boil.

This period taught me much about myself and something about investing. We can't separate ourselves into two personas — the self who is an investor and the self who is the product of all our experiences. Our investment decisions are not made in a vacuum.

I learned two main things at this time in my career:

- I get incredibly nervous with direct equity holdings and feel much more comfortable if I don't make the underlying portfolio decisions.
- I tend to overanalyse my decisions as I seek to confirm I've made the right ones.

It's bloody exhausting! This is when I realised that a large part of investing is understanding what works for you and that success requires self-awareness. Investing was a means to an end for me. I had come to the realisation that it was something I needed to do, and I embraced its possibilities for my life. Yet even after investing for years it did not come naturally. It still made me anxious. I was an investor — but a reluctant one.

(continued)

Bringing it all together

Joining Morningstar helped trigger a shift in mindset as I came to see the bigger picture. I started investing because I saw the possible long-term outcomes. I still hadn't properly defined why I was investing.

I didn't know it at the time, but on reflection I can see I was in bunker mode, trying to increase my financial security in whatever way I could on a salary that didn't go very far in a city as expensive as Sydney. My focus had been on financial survival. I was earning enough to cover my expenses and put aside a little for my future, but not enough to think long term.

As my career progressed, my income grew and my perspective broadened. I had the opportunity to think beyond financial survival. I could set goals for myself—not just financial goals, but also personal ones for the kind of life I wanted to create.

I know some readers may interpret the lesson of my story to be that investing is only for people who have gotten ahead and already started to make money. That couldn't be further from the truth. Starting to invest small amounts when I was still on a low salary created a foundation that, through compounding, will make a big difference in my life.

The moral of my story is: don't delay investing. Get started as soon as possible using the techniques we've outlined. When I got to Morningstar, I started to see the value of planning. Having clear goals gave me not only a sense of purpose but also peace of mind. Instead of worrying about whether I was doing enough, whether I was on track, I followed a roadmap. I knew where I wanted to go, and I could start using the resources I had to give myself a better chance of getting there.

A large part of this is thinking about what I wanted my life to look like. That's a hard question for a young person. The foundation of my goals was my desire for independence and the confidence that comes from knowing I could take care of myself regardless of external influences. I wanted to travel and explore, and I wanted to live a life that made me happy.

Earning more money certainly helped broaden my perspective on what was achievable, but setting goals and planning gave me the confidence to achieve them.

Structure and define goals

I have long-term and medium-term goals. My first long-term goal is having a more than comfortable retirement. I want financial security and the ability to spend my time in a way that will be enriching. I am lucky that I took my retirement seriously from a young age and have a healthy superannuation balance that will continue to grow.

My second long-term goal is to travel comfortably.

There are a lot of uncertainties surrounding planning your retirement and the further you are away from it the greater the uncertainty. How can you know how much you'll need in retirement given you don't know how long you'll live? You can't know how the long-term inflation rate will impact the purchasing power of your money, or whether superannuation legislation will change in the decades before you retire (it likely will), or whether you will have chronic illnesses to manage.

Having a goal is essential. It's important to start somewhere and adjust as the picture of your retirement becomes clearer as you move towards it. For me, I know I'll want to travel. It's a common goal for many of us. I want to ensure that I have enough saved to fund my expenses and to enjoy travelling. My goals extend to preparing for the onset of chronic illness, as it is more likely than not that I will experience that.

It should be noted that I have deliberately not combined my retirement goals with my husband's. I love him and I can't

(continued)

imagine a world where we won't be spending our retirement together. However, that is what most people say yet almost 50 per cent of couples separate.

For my financial independence and peace of mind, it is important for me to be able to at least have my retirement as a goal independent of my relationship.

Mark's investing goals

When I was young my parents gave me small gifts of shares for my birthday or Christmas. They picked out companies that sold goods and services I used, such as Nike. They explained I was now an owner of the company and every time someone bought a pair of Nike shoes a little bit of that profit was mine. Simplistic explanation? It is, but too many people forget investing in shares means owning part of a business.

These small gifts added up over time and by the time I got to university I had a small portfolio. It was at university that I decided — unwisely — that it was time for me to start investing on my own. My confidence in myself was unsurprising. It was the time of the dotcom bubble and investing seemed easy because everything was going up.

I did what many people did at that time and many people do today. I found shares to buy that everyone else thought were great. I would find a superficially compelling narrative and buy a company I knew next to nothing about. I put no effort into interrogating the narrative and understanding the company. And I didn't have the perspective to understand that if everyone else thought an investment couldn't miss, those expectations were already reflected in the share price.

Everything about the dotcom bubble turned out to be illusory. It was all just hype. So when the bubble turned into a bloodbath I searched for something more tangible. And there isn't any part of investing that is more tangible than a dividend. Many people gravitate towards an income strategy as they approach retirement. Mine started before I even had a career. I became an income investor at university.

What mattered to me most was cash flow: the cash flow needed to pay a dividend and the cash flow a dividend provided. By the time I graduated dividends had become my obsession. It allowed me to measure progress in a way that made sense.

My account balance would go up and down as the market fluctuated. At first, I tracked my returns closely against an index. But there was something deeply dissatisfying about this method of judging my investment success. If the market fell by 10 per cent and my portfolio fell by 8 per cent it was a good result. However, it felt deeply detached from building a portfolio that would provide me with financial freedom, and that was my goal.

Early in my career I didn't like my job, so my goal was to retire early. I figured the simple way to do that was to grow my passive income to the point where I could live on it. This was my first experience with setting a goal. At the time I didn't understand why goal setting was so important, but it helped me to figure out what was possible and when I could retire. Since I was trying to achieve a certain level of income I measured my goal in passive income. I would model out different scenarios with my savings and look at the different sources of income growth, including reinvesting dividends to buy more shares and earn more dividends.

(continued)

As my career advanced my goals began to shift. It turns out that work is less monotonous as you progress and get new responsibilities. I started to think more about the type of life I wanted to live right now and not simply to focus on the future. I had saved religiously and built up my passive income and it was time to spend some of it.

My goals are fairly simple right now. I have a retirement goal for savings that go into super. Then I have income goals to improve my life incrementally by spending my passive income on travel. I set my income goals in five-year increments. Once I reach my goal, I add that passive income to what I spend on travel. For instance, my current goal is to generate a certain amount of passive income in one of my accounts by the time I reach 50. As soon as I reach that goal, I will set a new goal for 55.

I think setting goals in five-year increments is helpful. It's a short enough period that I have a reasonably accurate idea of how much I can save. It's helpful to keep reaching your goals because the sense of accomplishment is motivating. In my case, I get the added bonus of more travel at the goal's realisation. Using passive income as my goal instead of an account balance helps me avoid mistakes by overreacting to market movements. This approach works for me.

I am spending a portion of my passive income and that slows growth in my net worth. According to Hartford Funds and Ned Davis Research, since 1960, 85 per cent of the total return of the S&P 500 Index has come from dividends. Spending my passive income is reducing the growth I will experience, but I am okay with this trade-off. Over time my account balances continue to grow and since I'm not spending any of the principal, it will be available in the future.

Growing my cash flow is a better indication of my progress towards financial freedom so that's my goal and how I measure success. I tracked the growth in my income stream. I looked at how much my income was increasing through dividend reinvestment, dividend increases and new savings. This allowed me to be relaxed about how the market was performing. Soon I found myself actually hoping the market would drop. It meant my dividend reinvestment and new contributions brought me more income because the dividend yield went up as the market fell.

I had inadvertently stumbled on a way to remove behavioural risk from my investing. Not only did I not panic during a market drop – I welcomed it. To this day I think it is one of my primary sources of edge or competitive advantage as an investor.

Income investing may not be the right goal for you, but everyone needs goals. The goals should reflect what you want to accomplish in life and your money philosophy. That makes it more likely you will sacrifice to achieve your goal.

Key takeaways

Goals provide structure for decision making, which reduces the mistakes investors often make. Having a goal is motivating and makes it more likely you will achieve it.

Goal setting was the first big exercise of the book. Great job for getting through it. You've defined a goal by going through the process of costing it and calculating the return needed to achieve it. Your plan is starting to come together. You know how much you need to save and the return you need to earn, and this knowledge will inform your asset allocation and your investment strategy. This is a big step towards creating a personalised plan for financial freedom.

A new way of thinking about risk

We are creating a roadmap to guide you to financial independence. You will learn new things and add structure to the way you make decisions, and you will unlearn things you have picked up that are unhelpful. The way you should think about risk likely involves unlearning some things.

The Cambridge Dictionary defines risk as 'the possibility of something bad happening'. For professional investors that something is volatility, and volatility refers to prices — or the value of a portfolio — bouncing around.

When we think about something bad happening to our portfolio, we're unlikely to be worried about volatility. Our portfolio doesn't exist in a theoretical world. It's made up of assets we will sell in the future to pay for things we want and need, and until we sell them these assets are just numbers on a screen. On one level the risk we face is not having enough money in the future, but the real risk is not getting what we want out of life. We believe that for most investors risk has little to do with volatility.

What is the difference between the risk you see and the risk a professional investor sees? In large part it has to do with informational asymmetry. A professional fund manager investing on behalf of a large group of people doesn't know anything about those investors, their goals or their timelines. The manager defines high-level parameters for both volatility and return targets for a fund. It's up to the end investor or an intermediary such as an adviser to align goals and investments.

The professional fund manager's approach is the best we can hope for in an imperfect situation. But knowing what you want to accomplish gives you a huge advantage over a professional fund manager. You can design a portfolio that is right for you. You can worry about volatility when volatility is actually a problem, such as when you are approaching retirement. And you can consider your investments as part of your holistic financial situation. This means you can focus on the real risk of not achieving your goal.

The most important risk for investors

The way you build your portfolio will be shaped by what we think is the most important risk you face: not achieving your goals. You'll select different asset classes such as cash, bonds and stocks. The decision at the heart of portfolio construction is the choice of which asset classes to include and how much of each. This process is informed by comparing the risk and return requirements needed to accomplish your goal with the risk and return expectations of each asset class. This may sound complicated, but we are going to break it down into steps.

You have already calculated the returns you need to accomplish your goals. This is the foundation for considering risk as we've defined it. As we've said, we think about risk differently from most of our colleagues in the financial industry, who use terms such as *price volatility* and *standard deviation* as measures of risk. These measures are concerned with how much the price of an investment will fluctuate. This works well if you are focused on your investment but less well when you're focused on your goals.

One thing you will read repeatedly in this book is that the key to achieving financial independence is shifting the focus from the investment to the investor. That's you. Let's do that again now by using our simpler and more practical application of the term risk as failing to meet your goals — of not having enough money in time to retire when you'd planned to or having to change your lifestyle to make your savings last.

In the spirit of calling a spade a spade, we will refer to risk as the risk you won't meet your goals, and volatility as the risk your portfolio's value will temporarily move around. Take some time to think about your own view of risk and how fluctuations in your portfolio could affect your life. If you are investing for the long term and can adequately cover any short-term cash outlays with an emergency fund, then perhaps your definition of risk is the same as ours.

As an example, we can look at someone who is hoping to retire in 15 years. This person has, like you, calculated the rate of return needed to achieve their goal. To hit their retirement number they need a 3 per cent real return (after inflation) or a 5.6 per cent nominal return (before inflation).

This person talks to a friend at a party. The friend is excitedly discussing the 3.5 per cent nominal return term deposit she has just bought. She is happy with this return and couldn't imagine investing in the stock market because it goes up and down all the time. That sounds too risky. She has taken on the industry definition of risk. She is worried about volatility: she sees the stock market as risky because prices fluctuate.

But the term deposit just doesn't have a high enough return to meet your retirement goal. To listen to the friend means removing all risk from your portfolio, as it is defined by the financial services industry. Yes, a term deposit has no volatility. It won't bounce around in price and your friend will get back the money she put in plus some interest. But to buy such a term deposit would be to guarantee not meeting your retirement goal. Given your 15-year time horizon, your decision should be easy.

The risk-tolerance questionnaire

The friend's view of risk is similar to that of many in the industry. There are regulatory hoops with financial advice that make understanding your tolerance to risk a mandatory part of the financial planning process. This is almost always done through a risk-tolerance questionnaire (RTQ).

The use of a risk-tolerance questionnaire is common practice in financial advice firms, robo-advice and even self-help tools for new investors. It does what it says on the box. It is short — usually eight to ten questions — and is supposed to measure how much risk you can tolerate; that is, the degree of volatility you can withstand when it comes to investing. Based on your answers, you'll be assigned an asset allocation that is appropriate to your risk tolerance.

There are several issues with this approach. We have a philosophical disagreement with it that we will discuss in the next section of this chapter, but the basic problem is that many RTQs don't accurately measure risk tolerance. A research paper published by Baeckstrom, Marsh and Silvester (2020) shows that industry views of risk tolerance can significantly impact outcomes. Their research looked at gender disparity in the allocation of aggressive assets in portfolios.

Although it showed that clients who engage a financial adviser invest 10.6% more, men and women achieve different results. This is less about gender disparity and more about whether the risk-tolerance questionnaire is fit for purpose without additional context. Men and women, overall, have similar financial goals so why the disparity in portfolio allocation?

That women are more risk-averse is reflected in their portfolios. Women held 5 per cent more cash in their portfolios than men even though they had the same levels of investment knowledge and confidence as men. Women who had selected male advisers increased their cash holdings on average by 13.4 per cent and reported they felt less knowledgeable about their decisions. The results of the study suggest the definition of risk the industry applies to individual investors is skewed to risk aversion. It's about how an individual feels about volatility and this drives asset allocation, which significantly impacts outcomes. Instead, the focus should be on financial goals. Given these goals are unlikely to be that different for men and for women, the approaches shouldn't be that different either.

We can see this mismatch, too, when we look at the superannuation system. AustralianSuper is Australia's largest superfund and 90 per cent of members are in the Balanced PreMixed option. Many of these investors are equating risk with volatility and not with the risk of not achieving their goals. The balanced option holds more than 24 per cent of the fund in defensive assets.

Of course every individual is different, but it is obvious to us that many of the more than 3 million people in the balanced option are investing too conservatively.

Over the past 10 years, the AustralianSuper High Growth option has delivered annualised returns of 9.04 per cent, while the Balanced option has delivered returns of 8.07 per cent. For investors contributing $10k a year over 35 years, the difference is significant. The investor in the Balanced option would have a balance of $1 750 244, while the investor in High Growth would have $2 176 748. That's almost 25 per cent more in retirement savings.

Shani says ...

Statistically, women are more risk-averse. They have higher savings, but lower investing rates. I am a risk-averse person. At the same time, I find the risk of losing financial independence and security a much tougher scenario than worrying about the volatility of my investments. I've also realised that I'm not a hobbyist investor. Picking winners and monitoring investments is not something I enjoy, so the hurdle for me is getting invested and staying invested. This means I've naturally gravitated towards diversified investments where volatility is lower than with a single stock. This suits my temperament as an investor and ensures I stay invested for the long run.

How a risk-tolerance questionnaire works

As we have previously pointed out, it is difficult to anticipate how you will react in an emotional environment and it's one in which many investors make poor decisions. That makes it unlikely that a risk-tolerance questionnaire will accurately assess your future actions. Here is an example of a question from a risk-tolerance questionnaire distributed by a large financial services firm:

You have an initial investment portfolio worth $100 000. If your portfolio fell to $85 000 within a month, would you:

• sell all of the investments
• sell a portion of your portfolio to cut your losses and reinvest into more secure investments
• hold the investment and sell nothing, expecting performance to improve
• invest more funds to lower your average investment price?

The problem we see with this is, first, the situation is hypothetical. None of us truly knows how we will react in a stressful situation. For us, the logical answer is the last option. We have long time horizons, stable salaries and are not reliant on investment income. We can afford to wait for markets to recover.

In previous market drops, we have averaged down most of the time. But sometimes we've also just held the investment and sold nothing (the third option).

Another problem with focusing on your risk tolerance is that it has nothing to do with your investment goals. An asset allocation selected based on your risk tolerance and not the return you need to achieve is blind to your goals. As we see investing as a means to an end a risk tolerance–based investment approach is a good way not to get what you want out of life.

These questionnaires are typically short, because whoever is trying to measure risk tolerance knows people don't want to answer a lot of questions. They want to get to the fun part of investing, which is deciding what to buy. A more cynical view is that whoever is setting the RTQ wants to get to the profitable part of the process, which is selling investments.

This issue relates to something called the Spearman-Brown Prophecy, which attempts to test the connections between questionnaire length and the reliability of results. The goal is to design tests that are comprehensive enough to be accurate. Roszkowski, Davey and Grable reported in a 2005 article in the *Journal of Financial Planning* that to achieve a reliable rate of accuracy, typically given a reliability estimate of .80, requires 25 questions.

Another issue is that perceptions of risk change. They change based on what is happening in the world. For example, the same researchers noted how, unsurprisingly, the perception of risk changed after the global financial crisis. Your perceptions may also change based on your mood and age.

The accuracy of RTQs has been extensively studied. We think it reasonable to conclude that some are better than others and a questionnaire administered by a good financial adviser as part of a comprehensive financial advice process can offer a better picture of risk tolerance than one administered hastily. We also think there is a better way.

Is there another way?

Risk capacity is the amount of risk an investor needs to take on to reach their financial goals. And here is the key difference. Risk tolerance does not take into account what you actually need to do if you are to achieve your goals; it only considers your reaction if markets fall. Ultimately, if you are only taking risk tolerance into account, whether or not you reach your goals is entirely up to chance.

We acknowledge that investments are volatile and that volatility needs to be managed. An investment is simply a vehicle to assist us in reaching our goals. That may mean taking on more volatility than we feel comfortable with.

Your reframed view of risk

Reframing risk and disassociating it from volatility is an important exercise for long-term investors. That reframing means your investment allocation is about you and what you want to achieve. This doesn't mean that volatility isn't hard on investors. We have both lived through periods in which we have watched our portfolios drop day after day. We've experienced that sense of powerlessness.

As the pressure builds and is reinforced by your friends, family and the media, it becomes harder to resist selling. It would be so easy to relieve the pressure. All you have to do is sell and all the fear goes away.

Morningstar's annual 'Mind the Gap' report shows how, during times of market volatility, the gap between total investor returns and actual returns increases, as does poor investor behaviour.

There's no magic bullet to help you deal with volatility, which allows so many in the financial services industry to preach that investors should allow risk tolerance to dictate their investment approach even when it means they risk not achieving their goals. But we have more faith in everyday investors. We think education helps so that is the driver of this book, and our jobs. Knowing the trade-offs and the 'why' behind the decisions you make will help you stick to your plan when the market falls. Structure, as we explain in this book, helps too. Structure curbs impulsive behaviour and reduces the impact of the emotional ride that is the sharemarket.

How do investors understand their risk capacity?

The good news is you have already assessed your risk capacity — just review our goal-setting process. You know your investment destination. You know how much to save and what return you need. Without this knowledge it would be impossible to design a successful investment strategy.

The required rate of return you calculated in the previous chapter is your guide to selecting your asset allocation, the mix of defensive and growth assets that will enable you to reach your financial goals.

We know from experience that investors can improve their behaviour once they have the necessary knowledge. Understanding the benefits of higher returns that come from accepting volatility over the long term will provide ballast when markets inevitably zig and zag. By going through the process we've prescribed, you will be able to focus on your long-term goal instead of fluctuating prices. The portfolio construction process you have undertaken will provide a level of understanding about the relationship between risk and reward that a risk-tolerance questionnaire could never do.

One of the biggest challenges an investor faces is focusing on the long term and not responding to emotions aroused by volatility. The issue with an RTQ is that it focuses only on how an investor responds over the short term and isn't oriented to long-term goals. A good financial adviser combines the questionnaire with context of their client's life, responsibilities and future goals. We are helping you go through that same process. This is the key to aligning the investments in your portfolio with the outcomes you are looking to achieve.

Mark says ...

I try to keep myself grounded in foundational investing concepts. Investing is a trade-off between risk and reward. In investment-speak risk is volatility or how much an asset bounces around in price in the short term. When it comes to riskier assets like shares, we exchange that short-term volatility for higher expected returns over the long term. The key words here are *long term*. If I want to achieve high returns from shares consistently, I need to hold them for long time periods so short-term drops in price can be counteracted.

There are other benefits as well. I will likely pay less tax. I will pay less in transaction costs, which include both brokerage and the buy–sell spread. Long holding periods afford me the opportunity to reinvest dividends. That has a compounding effect on not just the number of shares I hold but also the income generated from my portfolio in the future. Far outweighing these other benefits is the likelihood that longer holding periods result in fewer mistakes.

The rationalisations that lead to frequent trading are often simply justifications to make decisions that hurt long-term performance. It may seem rational to sell because the market seems 'risky'. It may seem rational to sell a position to buy the new ETF with the slick marketing campaign or to follow the advice of a mate who is pitching a can't-miss share. But these rationalisations are often just cover for chasing performance.

Exercise: Reframing risk

It is easy for us to say that investors should ignore volatility. Intellectually it makes complete sense to focus on risk capacity rather than risk tolerance. Yet we know investors still make more mistakes when markets are volatile.

Throughout this book we have two goals. We want to provide the structure to clearly point to risk capacity as your primary concern. This was the purpose of the goal-setting exercise in the previous chapter. We also want to reframe your view of risk to dampen the impact of volatility on your emotions. It doesn't mean you won't react emotionally to volatile markets, but it does give you the intellectual framework to resist the temptation to act.

To change your risk mindset, think about reframing a common question on the RTQ. Would your answer change if, instead of 'Could you tolerate a 20 per cent swing in your portfolio?', a questionnaire were to ask, 'Could you tolerate a 20 per cent swing in your portfolio if that were the only way to achieve your goals?'? We think most people would accept that trade-off.

Write down each of the risks to achieving your financial goals. You can refer specifically to each of your goals now that you've defined them. They include a savings target and an average return you need to achieve your goal. Think about ways your goals could be derailed.

We suspect the risks you write down won't be related to volatility. Perhaps you've listed losing your job so you can't save or earning a lower salary. Perhaps an unexpected expense could reduce your ability to save. Not earning a high enough return is likely to pose a risk. But in that case responding to volatility will probably do more harm than good, regardless of the emotions you feel.

Keep a copy of this list of risks to your goals. Remind yourself of them every time you are worried about your portfolio.

Mark's reaction to a bear market

I am a firm believer that many investors' concerns about volatility hold them back from achieving their financial goals. Yet I also know how hard it is to live through a bear market. The most challenging investing period I have faced was the global financial crisis (GFC), which began in 2007.

What is missing from many accounts of bear markets is what else is going on outside the market itself. Investors are people and we react not just to what is happening to our portfolios but also to things happening in our life.

During the GFC I was a management consultant living in Boston. I worked with large financial institutions — the very firms that were collapsing or at the least struggling to stay in business. It was not a great time to be a consultant.

As I watched my portfolio drop, I also faced job insecurity. My boss was laid off, along with the person directly under me. It wasn't a leap to imagine I would be next. Bear markets don't happen in isolation, and the pressure of seeing your portfolio fall isn't likely to be the only thing on your mind.

Experience has taught me a few things that can be helpful when it comes to negotiating bear markets. The first is to have a plan and a strategy you believe in. The confidence necessary for investing for the long term comes from knowing what you're doing and why you're doing it. This extends to the holdings in your portfolio. You need to understand and believe in the investments you own and why each holding is going to help you achieve your goal. If you own something just because you're sure it will go up in price, what happens when it doesn't? That's when investors sell.

The second way to survive a bear market is to understand that it's a dangerous time for investors, not just because your

(continued)

investments go down in value but also because your decision making suffers. Just knowing I'm more likely to make mistakes during bear markets reminds me to really interrogate my decision making.

You'll recall Morningstar's 'Mind the Gap' study and its comparison of the returns on funds and ETFs with the returns for the investors who have owned those funds and ETFs.

Investor returns are influenced by the timing of buy-and-sell decisions. The gap between investment and investor returns is an indication of how poor we are at making decisions. Each poor decision is a point of failure. The most recent 'Mind the Gap' study found the cumulative impact was a 1.60 per cent gap between investment returns and investor returns over the previous decade. Collectively investors are not up to the challenge in the best of times.

Given this is an annual study, the size of the gap will fluctuate each time we run a new set of data. Over time we've noticed several patterns. The gap widens when there is more volatility. This is evident when different types of investments have different levels of volatility — say, share ETFs and bond ETFs. The investor gap is bigger for share ETFs than bond ETFs. It is also bigger when different time periods have different levels of volatility. For instance, in 2019 the gap was around 1 per cent; in 2020 the turbulence around COVID widened the gap to close to 2 per cent.

This makes sense. Volatility is driven by lots of investors making decisions. Some are pulling money out of the market, and some are putting money in. In 2020 there was a rapid drop followed by an immediate rally. Overall, each market timing decision by an investor lowers returns. In a year when more decisions are made, returns are lower.

I want to be clear about what happened and what the data is telling us. Given how dramatic and rapid the COVID bear market and rally were, it is a good laboratory in which to investigate poor behaviour.

The market drop occurred over 33 days, between February 19 and March 23. At some point during that drop many investors decided to sell. This was followed by a furious rally. At some point during the rally many investors decided to buy.

Often these sellers and buyers were the same people. If investors had done nothing and just held on throughout the drop and subsequent rally, they would have been 2 per cent better off, but they didn't do this. And despite their best intentions they didn't buy low and sell high. To do nothing is often the smartest approach.

The final thing that helps is simply to maintain an emergency fund. Having cash available always gives me confidence that I can make it through whatever the market throws at me.

What a risk-tolerance questionnaire tells Shani to invest in

I completed a risk-tolerance questionnaire that concluded that my married status meant I could take on less risk than if I were single. It also suggested a conservative allocation because I had never borrowed money to invest before. These two facts may indicate a lower willingness to take risk, but they have nothing to do with how much risk I should take.

Ultimately the questionnaire placed me in the balanced category. Balanced tells me to take on 50 per cent growth assets, and 50 per cent defensive assets and has a minimum time horizon of five years.

(continued)

But I have almost 40 years until I retire. I do not need to hold half my portfolio in defensive assets. My portfolio may go up and down over the short term, but ultimately that doesn't really matter since I won't need the money for decades. I am very confident of this because I've built up an emergency fund — something the questionnaire didn't ask about.

I've defined my goals, and the rate of return I will need for the retirement I want. That return is higher than a balanced portfolio offers me. I am risk-averse. The questionnaire got that part right. Yet to follow the questionnaire's advice would mean not achieving my goals. To me that doesn't sound like a good trade-off.

Key takeaways

Risk is one of the most misunderstood concepts in investing, and framing risk incorrectly can lead you down a path where you fail to achieve your goals. Risk tolerance speaks to how comfortable you are with risk. Risk capacity focuses on what you need to achieve your goals. Because we believe the biggest risk is not achieving your goals, we think investors should focus on risk capacity.

Creating a goal provides all the inputs you need to start thinking about risk capacity rather than risk tolerance. This matters if you are to invest successfully. But your mindset around risk also matters. Writing down the real risks to achieving your goals may help persuade you that short-term volatility is not what you need to worry about. You can also refer back to this list when market movements are making you anxious.

Don't put all your eggs in one basket

There are few investing topics as boring as diversification. 'Diversify' is the universal advice of investment advisers and all manner of investing commentators, though there's at least one investor who has a different take. Warren Buffett argues that diversification 'is a protection against ignorance' but that 'it makes little sense if you know what you are doing'.

This advice could be used by investors to justify speculative and risky behaviour, but that isn't how we see it. We agree that investors draw some questionable conclusions from the standard talking points about diversification. We think the reason is most investors don't bother thinking about it at a deeper level. This leads to confusion around its importance as well as how to go about it.

To figure out how to use diversification to achieve your goals, we'll start with the basics.

The arguments against diversification

Just because we don't think people are thoughtful about diversification doesn't mean we think people shouldn't diversify. Many of the arguments against diversification don't hold up to scrutiny.

The key to achieving the best return possible is to pick the best-performing share and put all your money into it. Good luck. This is obviously easier said than done.

Yet that is the basic argument often made when arguing against diversification. The proponents of a concentrated portfolio cite studies looking at how wealth is accumulated. It's true that the wealth of most self-made investors comes from concentrated holdings in a single company. The caveat is that those who have amassed wealth in this way typically either started the company themselves or own a controlling stake.

A founder and/or controlling shareholder is very different from the minority shareholders who make up the majority of investors in the sharemarket. Later we will explore the four sources of edge or competitive advantage an investor can have. One of these, information edge, involves outperforming other investors by knowing something they don't. That seems obvious.

There was a time when some minority shareholders could have this edge, but it has largely been eliminated by regulation — rules about what information a company may disclose and how. This ensures equal access to information for all shareholders.

These rules don't impact a majority shareholder who still runs a company. It's a given that they'll know more about it than other shareholders. And the fact that they started and grew a successful company means they also know the industry and the competitive dynamics better than many other people.

We are advocates for knowing about the companies you own, but it's important to recognise you will never be able to research your way into knowing everything.

A month and a half before Enron's bankruptcy, 12 out of 15 analysts had a strong buy rating on the company's shares. In some ways Enron was a special case, as its management engaged in fraud, but it does illustrate why running a concentrated portfolio is a risk.

Some experts believe there were red flags while others argue it's very difficult to get wind of deliberate fraud. The more important question to ask yourself is do you have the knowledge, time and temperament to identify issues in financial statements and go against the crowd by acting on your suspicions? We know we don't.

There are risks other than fraud to be aware of. The global pandemic shut down large parts of the economy. Very few people foresaw the COVID scenario or how it would impact their portfolio.

A combination of disparate and often unpredictable factors sometimes coincide to impact companies. War, new technology, management greed and poor decision making are examples. If something can go wrong at some point it probably will.

This is the lens we will apply to diversification. We believe there is always a risk that a company will blow up. If that company makes up too much of your portfolio you might not be able to achieve your goals, which is of course the risk you should be protecting yourself from.

How likely are catastrophic losses?

Recognising the likelihood of a catastrophic loss will help reinforce the need to diversify. JP Morgan's 2021 study *The Agony and the Ecstasy* explores this topic. Its focus is the Russell 3000 index, which represents the entire US stock market. The researchers found that 40 per cent of all stocks suffered a permanent 70 per cent plus decline from their peaks. These companies never traded again at more than a 60 per cent loss from their peak.

The return on the median stock in the Russell 3000 compared with the index was −54 per cent. Two-thirds of all shares underperformed against the index. For 40 per cent of shares in the index, their absolute returns were negative.

Read that again. It is sobering. JP Morgan's study focused on the losers but there is also research on the winners. Professor Hendrick Bessembinder's extensive research into the US sharemarket explored how many shares create shareholder value — that is to say they exceed the return on short-term US Government Treasury Bills.

Bessembinder's 2018 study covered 26 000 US listed companies between 1926 and 2016. Only 90 companies account for half of all shareholder wealth. That's one-third of 1 per cent of the total number of listed companies. The top 4.3 per cent, just over 1000 companies, account for all shareholder wealth. Moreover, 96 per cent of all US listed shares had a return equal to or below the US Government Treasury Bill rate.

The theory of diversification

Each asset class has a distinct risk–return profile. To a lesser extent the underlying sectors and geographies within an asset class also have different risk–return profiles — for instance, Australian shares and US shares. However, in times of crisis markets tend to move together.

As investors we are compensated for taking on volatility. Typically, the more volatile an investment the higher the long-term returns. We've stressed that we don't think most investors should consider volatility a risk. Yet when someone refers to a risk–return profile they are measuring the trade-off between volatility and long-term returns. After reading this book your focus should be on the trade-off between the long-term returns of a particular asset and the return you need to achieve your goal.

As we discussed in the previous chapter, the investment industry considers volatility the main risk and there are measures to express the degree of volatility. Two popular ones are *standard deviation* and *beta*. These can be confusing for many investors. Some don't know what they mean; others aren't sure how to use them.

Once again, a cynical view is that the confusion is designed by the investing industry to reinforce the notion that investing is best left to a professional who understands standard deviation and why it matters. A more generous take is that these terms are useful if you are managing large pools of investor money and aren't focused on the goals of the investors who make up that pool. We believe most investors can ignore these volatility measures. We think it is more productive to focus on the long-term return potential of different asset classes in relation to your goal and to prepare yourself mentally to ignore short-term volatility.

There are specific situations in which volatility is a real risk. Typically, that is as investors are approaching their goal. It can be devastating if a large decline in value occurs right before you need your investments to pay for your goal. Think about the impact of a big drop in the market on your goal. Ask yourself what the impact on your life would be if you couldn't attain your goal until the market recovered. If the impact is large, it would make sense to move into less volatile investments or even into cash.

This once again demonstrates why it's so important to have a personalised plan. Using a universal definition of a risk such as volatility makes no sense when it only impacts a segment of the investing population. As a long-term investor you should be less concerned with how much your portfolio is going to bounce around in value and more concerned about whether or not your portfolio has been designed to give you a reasonable chance to achieve your goal. That is the real risk you face.

Balancing diversification and concentration

The importance of diversification is one of the first lessons investors learn. It has been called the 'only free lunch' in investing. However, overdiversification can lead to diluted returns. There must be a balance between diversification and concentration risk.

Concentration risk is the equivalent of putting too many of your eggs in one basket. As Australians, many of us are too concentrated in the Aussie market. Exacerbating this risk, the Australian stock market is concentrated on two main industries — financial services and mining. Further, we derive income from the Australian economy. All of a sudden, we have most of our super and investments in the Australian economy and our income is derived from the Australian economy. This is one example of concentration risk. Other examples would be concentrating your investments in one particular manager, or in one investment, such as a house.

It is an understatement to say Australians are obsessed with property. Houses come up whenever investing and personal finance are discussed. Unaffordability, the best places to buy and how to get into the market are common themes. Many Australians' wealth is concentrated in the illiquid asset that is their primary place of residence, and according to the ATO more than two million of us have further concentrated our wealth through investment properties.

A survey commissioned by Raiz Invest in 2019 suggests Australians have no problem with this: 53 per cent of participants don't believe cash is the safest place to invest money and 22 per cent believe property is the safest investment.

Whichever assets you hold, concentration is a risk for investors to manage. One of the main questions to ask: What is the balance between concentration and diversification? How many shares should I have in my portfolio?

Investors need to ask themselves, if the value of any investment or security dropped to zero, would it prevent me from reaching my goals? This is the risk you need to balance.

Many financial commentators and professionals see 12 to 18 stocks as a safe number because it diversifies the risk while maintaining enough concentration for each holding to have a decent impact on returns.

Mark says...

I generally ignore any suggestion that I should own a little bit of everything. I remove single security risk by limiting individual share holdings to less than 5 per cent of my portfolio. I also make sure that a single share doesn't provide more than

(continued)

5 per cent of the income generated from my portfolio. Other than that I don't think much about diversification. I'm happy to ignore regions of the world, sectors of the stock market and different asset classes if I'm not comfortable with them. I don't think it does me any good over the long term to own some obscure investment that may outperform from time to time.

Practical steps to building a portfolio

An academic example of a diversified portfolio will always contain a mix of many asset classes — cash, international and domestic fixed income, alternatives, international and domestic equities. Gold, crypto and commodities might be added to the mix. You can always find an argument to add another asset class in the interests of diversification.

In reality, such a complicated mix is often not necessary. Diversification is the process of removing single-security risk from a portfolio. Once that is accomplished, many investors pick and choose which asset classes and investments will best help them reach their goal.

The goal of removing single-security risk is not the justification you often hear for diversification. Instead, many in the investment industry like to talk about buying uncorrelated assets — that is to say, assets whose values don't move in lockstep. Taken to the extreme, holding negatively correlated assets means prices move in opposite directions.

The reason the investment industry talks up uncorrelated assets goes back to the idea that volatility is synonymous with risk. Uncorrelated assets lower volatility in a portfolio; a negatively correlated asset acts as a hedge. There may be very specific reasons why an investor would want to lower the volatility of a portfolio or hedge it. It shouldn't be the default move, however.

Remember, it is important to avoid the mindset that says being a great investor involves holding a complex portfolio. Being a great investor means you accomplish your goals. You don't lose any points for doing that in the simplest and safest way possible.

We think the benefits of simplicity outweigh those of complexity. Keeping track of a complex portfolio is time-consuming and rebalancing a complex portfolio can be difficult. Adding new contributions to your portfolio can be challenging as your holdings grow since you will need to decide where to funnel new savings.

As we've reiterated, most investors lower their returns by trading too much. More holdings increase the temptation to tinker, risking your goals.

Research from Morningstar shows that portfolio diversification doesn't have to be complicated. A simulation with a basic mix of 60 per cent stocks and 40 per cent investment-grade bonds was compared with a portfolio that held 11 different asset classes.

The more complex portfolio was made up of 20 per cent large-cap domestic shares, 10 per cent developed and emerging markets stocks, Government bonds, US core bonds, global bonds and high-yield bonds, and 5 per cent each in small-cap stocks, commodities, gold and real estate investment trusts (REITs). Although the more diversified portfolio outperformed at times, the 60/40 mix provided better risk-adjusted returns in about 87 per cent of the rolling 10-year periods since 1976.

This is great news because it means you don't have to overcomplicate your portfolio. It doesn't take much to achieve the right mix with adequate diversification. Your job is to find investments that will help you meet the return and asset allocation requirements that will achieve your goal. Your investment strategy will include security-selection criteria that provide a framework for picking from the thousands of available investment options.

One of the most common questions we get is about quantity. How many stocks should I have in my portfolio? How many ETFs? How many funds?

Let's start with ETFs and managed funds. A simple portfolio involves a single ETF for each asset class to which you want exposure. For most investors shares and a single defensive asset class such as bonds or cash will probably suffice. Aussie investors will typically want one ETF for Australian shares and one for global shares plus a defensive asset class.

An army of investors termed Bogleheads follow the advice of Vanguard founder John Bogle. He advocated for the simplicity of a three-ETF portfolio for the reasons we've outlined. A portfolio needn't be limited to just three ETFs but as an investor you should consider seriously the justification for adding any and every additional holding. It may make sense to do so based on your goals and investment strategy. Just be sure there is a high hurdle for including asset classes like emerging markets, small-cap shares, a thematic or factor ETF or any of the countless other offerings.

When it comes to equities, there are many professional investors and financial firms that provide guidance on how many shares are adequate for diversifying away risk. The number ranges from 12 to 30 but the number alone, without context, is meaningless. It's the shares themselves that matter — the sectors, industries, geography.

Consider this when picking the shares in your portfolio, especially in Australia with its concentration in the two industries of mining and financial services. Because Australian investors have a great sense of home bias — they like to focus on Australia — many of them are invested in one geography and mostly across two industries.

To sum up, don't overcomplicate your portfolio and do have your investments directly connected to the goals of your portfolio. You don't need a stake in every single asset class to be diversified.

Exercise: Diversification

You are on the pathway to a personalised investment strategy based on your goals. As part of your strategy, you will establish rules around diversification. A precursor is framing diversification around the goals you have already defined.

Start with asset classes. Think through which asset classes you want in your portfolio and why. We suggest you start high level and consider global and Australian shares, global and Australian bonds, global and Australian listed property and cash. You shouldn't just own something for the sake of owning something.

Look at the returns in different asset classes over the long term and compare them with the returns you need to achieve your goal. Think about the role you want an asset class to play in your portfolio and consider whether other options would achieve the same end, especially if they are cheaper to access or work better with the other assets in your portfolio. Write down which asset classes you will consider and which you won't, along with your rationale for these choices. This will be an input into setting your asset allocation as part of your investment strategy.

(continued)

Next move on to the individual holdings in your portfolio. If you use or plan to use funds or ETFs in your portfolio, this step is less critical. Funds and ETFs are already diversified, so you don't need to set a specific rule around holdings. It is perfectly reasonable to include one ETF or fund per asset class in your portfolio.

If you hold or plan to hold individual shares, there are other considerations. Think through position sizing or the percentage of your total portfolio that each share can make up. The risk you are trying to diversify away is that of not achieving your goal. Use that as the basis for your decision making. If a position that makes up 5 per cent of your portfolio were to go to zero, could you still achieve your goal? If not, that holding is too large.

One trick to help you as you complete this exercise is to go back to the calculation of your required rate of return. Don't change any of the other variables but reduce your current portfolio size by different amounts that represent size limits of a position. How much would it change your required rate of return if you were to reduce your current portfolio by 5 per cent? Could you make up for this change by saving more money to maintain the current required rate of return?

You don't need an exact number. Aim for a comfortable range for an individual share as a percentage of your portfolio while protecting your goal from a catastrophic loss. Write down the range for each position and your rationale for selecting it. This will be an input later.

Finally, consider any other aspects of your goal that may influence diversification. For instance, if you are an income investor you may want to limit the amount of income that comes from any one share. Think through any other components of diversification that are related to your individual goal.

Shani's focus on diversification goes beyond the standard advice

I think it is important to have exposure to global shares in my portfolio because the Australian sharemarket makes up a small portion of the overall global market and is concentrated in the banking and mining industries.

Global exposure can be achieved in more than one way. You could invest in a company trading on an international exchange or an ETF/fund that contains international securities, or buy a domestic stock that operates globally. This last method is often ignored by investors although it provides underlying exposure to a variety of markets, which is the point of diversifying globally. It also happens to have some heavyweights in its corner.

John Bogle and Warren Buffett were proponents of this method of diversification. Both believed that investing in US companies would have enough diversification to provide the desired benefits.

Bogle explained these views in detail in his 1993 investor classic *Bogle on Mutual Funds: New Perspectives for the Intelligent Investor*. Buffett has stated simply that investors who direct 90 per cent of their assets to domestic equities and 10 per cent to treasury bonds will be sufficiently diversified.

I think this is just one example of thinking about what you are trying to accomplish with diversification and the different ways you can achieve your goal. The goal of investing globally is to capitalise on the economic growth rates of different countries, but this doesn't mean you need to own companies that trade on the exchanges of each country you want exposure to.

Mark's diversification nightmare

I learned the downside of concentration during the global financial crisis. The largest position in my portfolio going into 2007 was Citigroup. And large is a bit of an understatement. It made up more than 15 per cent of my portfolio.

How did I find myself in this situation? My father-in-law spent his whole career at Citigroup. He generously gave Haley a couple of shares each year as a Christmas present. Over time they appreciated significantly. When we married and combined finances, there it was — 15 per cent of our portfolio in a single company.

I knew this was a bad idea. I would never build a position that large in my portfolio. And obviously I could have fixed the problem easily. The issue I confronted was that the shares had a very low-cost base. And I didn't want to pay the taxes on the capital gains.

Knowing I was doing something wrong but wanting to avoid the downside of making it right, I did something many of us do. I reasoned and justified my way out of my conundrum. I reasoned that I was young and I could fix this problem with time. I would save and invest more and that would slowly dilute the position. And this approach probably would have worked except that, as it turned out, I didn't have the luxury of time.

Heading into 2007 the US housing boom was going full steam ahead. And I knew something wasn't right. The signs of excess were everywhere. And while I didn't short the market and end up like a character in Michael Lewis's *The Big Short*, I was at the very least attuned to the risk.

I knew that banks like Citigroup were underwriting and buying mortgages to securitise them. This gave me confidence that if something went wrong and people started to default, it wouldn't matter because the mortgages had been sold. When it increases confidence, a little bit of knowledge can be dangerous. Especially when that incomplete knowledge masks the risk.

I justified my actions with the fact that Citigroup wasn't a pure investment bank. It was mostly a commercial bank with operations all around the world. Securitising mortgages was only a small part of their operations. And, after all, this was Citigroup, one of the largest banks in the world. Run by smart people and a sophisticated risk management team. A former Treasury Secretary, Robert Rubin, worked there. What could go wrong?

A lot, it turns out. The bank did securitise the mortgages and sold them to investors. That got them off the books. The detail about creating collateralised debt obligations (CDOs) is unimportant. The important point is that they kept the riskiest parts of the bonds they created because nobody wanted to buy them. They were willing to take on the risk because that is the only way they could earn the fees for creating the CDOs. Citigroup set up off-balance-sheet entities as a dumping ground.

They also warehoused a lot of the mortgages on their balance sheet while they created the CDOs. Eventually 80 per cent of those mortgages would default.

My assumption about a competent risk management function? I was partly right. Multiple risk officers raised red flags and warned senior management and the board about what was happening. At least someone identified the risks. The problem was that everyone who raised the alarm was either demoted

(continued)

or fired. The only thing I managed to accomplish by my mistake was avoid those capital gains taxes. Turns out there aren't many capital gains when a share goes down 97 per cent in 18 months.

Clearly there are lots of lessons to be learned here. I've changed my investment approach, and I focus on companies that are easier to understand. It is very difficult to ascertain all the risks lurking on the balance sheet of a bank.

Yet my mistake did not arise from ignorance alone. While I may not have known the risks lurking in Citigroup's balance sheet, I did know the risk of having such a large position in a single share. That I spent so much time justifying my lack of action attests to the fact that I knew I was doing something wrong. In a different world I likely would have gotten away with it. That didn't make it smart.

Life has a way of humbling everyone. All you can do is learn from your mistakes and move forward.

Key takeaways

The purpose of diversification is to protect you from risk. The risk to concentrate on is the risk of not achieving your goal. Using your goal as a measuring stick provides context to which asset classes to include in your portfolio based on their return and volatility profiles. The risk to your goal is also the basis for making a decision on how many individual holdings to include in your portfolio. Focus on what you are looking to accomplish from diversification; you don't have to own every asset class or every type of underlying investment.

The next major step after you've defined a goal is to create a personalised investment strategy. Your view on diversification is a key input as your investment strategy will outline the different asset classes you will invest in and contain rules around position-sizing and rebalancing. After completing the exercise in this chapter you will have a rationale for including and excluding different asset classes. If you choose to invest in individual shares, you will have also documented position-sizing ranges and any other types of diversification that relate to your personal goals. You are one step closer to your personal plan for financial freedom.

What success looks like

Just 30 kilometres outside of Philadelphia, Pennsylvania, sits the sleepy town of Malvern. Population: 3419. The town was best known as the site of the obscure battle of Paoli in the Revolutionary War, when British regulars surprised American militia in a night attack. The town is now known for something else: it is the headquarters of Vanguard, which manages just under A$14.8 trillion in assets. That's a hard number to wrap your head around. It's more than five times Australia's GDP. Vanguard could buy every publicly traded company in Australia — 8.75 times over. Vanguard is the champion of passive investing and has become synonymous with the investing style. As passive investing has gained in popularity, Vanguard has become a juggernaut in the investing world.

For years there has been a debate between advocates for active and passive management. It may be too early for either side to declare victory, but the momentum is certainly with passive. Investors will argue passionately about active versus passive. Within active management there will be advocates for certain strategies or approaches.

You won't get that from us. We don't think there is only one investment strategy. One of the tenets of this book is that there are multiple ways you can invest to accomplish your goals. We want you to find a strategy that you are comfortable with and believe in, that is right for your goals and your circumstances. That's why we think debating the 'right' strategy is of little value.

However, the debate on actively managed versus passively managed investments does illustrate where so many investors go wrong. In this chapter we dig into the debate a bit further to show that it isn't what you invest in that matters; it's how you invest and how you frame success.

Before getting back to passive investing, we need to consider the process you should go through to choose the investment approach that's right for you. It's all about what edge you will exploit to achieve your goals.

What is your edge?

Edge is one of those pieces of jargon that professional investors like to throw around. It refers to an advantage one investor has over other investors. Exploiting that edge can be a mechanism through which you achieve your goals.

There are lots of different ways to be a successful investor. Finding the approach that's best for you involves thinking about your competitive advantage as an investor. Many people think the decks are stacked against them given the resources, education and experience of professional investors. We don't believe that's true.

If you don't feel like you have an investing edge, you can successfully reach your goals by investing passively. Self-control is an edge. Your superpower can be saving consistently. Patience is an edge, and your competitive advantage can be letting compounding do its work. In fact, many of the qualities needed to build wealth are in short supply these days. Focusing on doing what others can't is a great way to get ahead. There are four primary sources of edge that investors can exploit.

Informational edge

Informational edge is having more information about a particular investment than most other investors. Having unique information enables better investing decisions. This is very different from being an informed investor. There are lots of informed investors. It's all about information availability, not the effort required to obtain it. If information is available to every investor who bothers to look for it, there can be no informational edge. Given changes in regulations over the years, this edge is hard to obtain legally. Acquiring the information illegally constitutes insider trading. It's unlikely, then, that anyone reading this book has an informational advantage.

Analytical edge

In this case, an investor has the same information as other investors but does a better job of drawing conclusions from that information. Our observation is that many investors believe they have analytical edge. We suspect that much of this belief is misguided. Obtaining analytical edge is very hard to do. Remember, you are not competing against your halfwit neighbour. You are competing against teams of highly educated and well-paid professional investors who spend all day analysing investments. You need to be consistently better than most investors — professional and individual — to have analytical edge. The investment industry sells analytical edge because that's the expertise you are supposedly paying for. This assumption of analytical edge as the key to success is misguided. You can be a very successful investor without analytical edge.

Behavioural edge

Successful investing is not just an intellectual exercise. It also involves holding emotions at bay when making decisions on when to buy and sell different investments. There are countless behavioural impediments to successful investing, and we've outlined the impact of poor decisions multiple times in this book. It's challenging to overcome ingrained biases, but changing your behaviour is possible and we feel strongly that this is a source of edge that any investor can have. Providing structure around decision making is key. This is the principle we are trying to instil throughout this book.

Structural edge

Structural edge refers to external factors that influence the way an investor acts. This is largely an issue for professional investors. We've tried to point out some of the many ways that a professional investor is different from an individual investor. There are lots of factors that influence professionals, including career considerations, dealing with investor inflows and outflows, and pressure to not let short-term performance dip below an index. None of these issues should impact you. One of the great things about being an individual investor is that we can focus on the long term and our individual objectives. Too many of us give up this advantage to follow professional investors and worry too much about the short term. This is another source of edge that non-professional investors can and should use to their advantage.

This book focuses on behavioural edge and structural edge. We think these are the two advantages that any investor can have. It doesn't matter how knowledgeable you are about investing or how much time you want to dedicate to managing your portfolio. You need only understand what impacts your ability to achieve your goal and put in place the right structure to maintain the consistency and patience needed to be successful. Most people don't do this, and the consequences can be profound.

Mark says ...

As a product of the American education system, I was presented with a copy of *The Catcher in the Rye* in sixth grade, like my peers across the country. The first time I read it was not the last, and I'm sure it will find its way into my hands again. The overriding theme of the book is hypocrisy. The young narrator, Holden Caulfield, loved pointing out the phoniness of adults. He was consumed by it. Holden would have had a field day with investors.

There's no better example of investor hypocrisy than the lip service paid to long-term investing. The benefits of long-term investing are universally acknowledged, and frequently proselytised by professional investors. Yet the data doesn't hold up.

Research from Morningstar showed that the average turnover ratio for US domestic equity funds in 2019 was 63 per cent. That means that every year more than half of the positions are new. And it isn't just professional managers who can't practise what they preach.

What most people do wrong

The reason you invest is to earn returns. Along with your savings, the returns you earn are the vehicle to get you from where you are to the goal you want to achieve. There is no feasible way for most people to achieve their goals without earning returns that meaningfully exceed inflation. The whole point of going through the goal-setting process is to figure out the returns you need to achieve your goal.

The problem is that many investors who go through the goal-setting process or even just instinctively know they need growth assets like shares sabotage themselves by frittering away those returns. To explore how this happens we can look at the theory behind passive investing and how many investors practise passive investing. This isn't an endorsement or indictment of passive investing. We think you should pick the best approach for you. Exploring passive investing provides some insights into how so many investors sabotage themselves.

Vanguard founder John Bogle described passive investing in a straightforward way. Pick your asset allocation. Gain exposure to each asset class using a broad-based index and then do nothing. The passive part about following Bogle's investment approach is not the investments in your portfolio — it's you.

You do nothing and trust that over the long term, low fees and better tax outcomes will make a difference. Trust that all this activity that investors go through making decisions on what to buy and sell and when to buy and sell only detracts from returns. Passive investing is based on the notion that investors can't make good decisions consistently and end up owning the wrong things at the wrong times. Bogle famously summed up passive investing like this: 'Don't look for the needle in the haystack. Just buy the haystack.'

This is a passive strategy. No-one is picking individual investments that go into a fund or ETF, and the end investor is not picking what to buy and sell or when to buy and sell those products.

This compelling investment approach has attracted legions of investors to the passive camp. The problem is that somewhere along the way people lost sight of why passive investing works. There's a difference between passive investing and using passive investment products to actively invest.

Buying and selling different passive investments is not passive investing. Stretching the boundaries of what is considered passive to narrower and narrower indexes that promise exposure to a compelling theme is not passive investing. Investing in products that follow an index with high turnover through constant rebalancing is not passive investing. Remember that the passive part of passive investing is not the products you buy. *You* are passive.

It isn't what you invest in but how you invest that matters

John Bogle was a big critic of ETFs when they came out. To Bogle an ETF didn't make any sense. If you are investing passively, why do you need an investment that you could easily trade? Bogle understood the downside of poor investor behaviour and was worried that the biggest selling point for an ETF — the fact that they are easy to trade — would lead to more trading. He was right. A study conducted by UTS in 2008 explored whether individual investors benefit from the use of ETFs. The study found that portfolio performance when investors used ETFs was lower than when they didn't.

It wasn't a small loss. The study found that ETF portfolios underperformed non-ETF portfolios by 2.3 per cent a year. In theory this makes no sense. The difference in returns is the result of buying and selling ETFs at the wrong time rather than choosing the wrong ETFs. A critical finding in the study was that ETF portfolios did outperform if the investor bought the investment and held it for the long term. Is there an inherent problem with ETFs? Of course not. The problem is us.

There is a difference between investments and investing. An investment is something you buy and sell, like an ETF or a share. Investing is a process. This book is about the process of investing. Most books about investing are about how to find the right investment to buy. We think the process is far more important. The success of any process comes down to a few common traits: patience, resilience and consistency lead the list. Investing is no different.

The inconvenient truth about investing is that our own behaviour is having a negative impact on our results. The good thing is that your behaviour is completely in your control. If you avoid mistakes, you will get better results than everyone else. Stop following the approach taken by many professional investors who frequently trade. They do that because if they have short-term underperformance investors will pull money out, which will hurt their livelihood. You have none of those pressures. The only thing trading too much is doing for you is hurting your returns.

Trading too much isn't just an issue with investors who pick passive investments. Active fund and ETF investors tell themselves that they are letting professionals manage their money because they think it's too hard to pick individual shares. Yet they constantly switch which professionals get to manage their money based on short-term performance.

Passive fund and ETF investors can be holier than thou. They quote John Bogle constantly, yet they don't follow his advice. They switch passive investments frequently based on their perception of what will do well based on short-term market conditions. They buy high and sell low. They decide anything tracking an index is passive, even if that index has 10 shares that are selected fortnightly using a Ouija board.

Both active and passive investing can work, but we don't think active investment works in the way it is practised by many fund managers. We also don't think passive investing works in the way most end investors practise it.

Our point is simple and is repeated ad nauseam throughout the book. In investing we have met the enemy ... and it is us. Changing your behaviour is hard. It means ignoring articulate people making compelling cases for and against investments. It requires immunity to highly paid and skilled marketers. It means dulling your emotions as your portfolio climbs and falls.

One of our favourite things about investing is that it is all about us. It's us against the world. Maybe the playing field isn't level and professionals have more time and resources than we do. Maybe they know more than we do. They may be far smarter than we are. Yet we retain control over our outcomes. It comes down to the basics: having a goal and a long-term strategy. Most of all, it means resisting the temptation to constantly chase returns.

Shani says...

Most investors believe that investing success requires finding the best investments. The foundation of this belief is that at any particular moment there are investments that are good and will outperform in the immediate future and ones that are bad that will underperform. This view is reinforced and encouraged by professionals who are selling investments and their ability to navigate markets to find opportunities.

(continued)

I've come to an approach that flips this conventional wisdom. Selecting individual investments for my portfolio is not my primary concern. I focus on factors in my control as I try to build wealth and achieve my goals. That means my savings, minimising taxes and fees, and limiting the impact of poor decisions on my investment approach.

What return are you getting?

We've spent a fair amount of time in this book quoting various studies that show how investors sabotage themselves with their actions. Now it's time to show why so many investors have poor results. There are lots of ways to turn a high market return into a low return in your brokerage account, and investors have found them all.

We talk to many investors and consume a lot of investing commentary. When investors and investing commentators talk about returns one number more likely than not will pop out. It has long been conventional wisdom that equity markets will return 10 per cent annually over the long run.

This isn't far from the truth. Since 1900 Australian shares have delivered returns of 13.20 per cent each year. Over the past 30 years returns have been 9.10 per cent per year. If we turn to US shares, the return since 1900 has been 9.94 per cent a year and 11.10 per cent over the past 30 years.

We need to dig a little deeper into that 10 per cent return. With a $100 000 initial investment and $1000 additional investments every month, in 20 years you would accrue $1 391 009 provided you reinvested dividends. However, this scenario ignores the reality of investing when returns are impacted by fees and taxes.

These factors need to be taken into account because what matters is how much money ends up in your account.

Understanding the holistic return increases your chance of reaching your financial goals. It also makes it more likely that you will pay attention to minimising taxes and fees.

Fees

Many people turn to funds and ETFs as an investment vehicle. There are a lot of advantages to this approach, but they do come with management fees. Even low fees can add up over the long term. If we assume a fee of 0.35 per cent a year, this will cost you $70 501 in our 20-year scenario. This drops the balance of your portfolio down to $1 320 508. There are many funds and ETFs with lower fees than our hypothetical example, but there are many with higher fees. The point is that fees matter and add up over time.

Brokerage

Brokerage costs differ from broker to broker. CommSec, the most popular broker in Australia, charges $5 for trades up to $1000.

This drops our return by $3446 to $1 317 062, assuming the only trades are buying new investments with the additional savings of $1000 every month. Most investors trade far more frequently.

Taxes

Taxes also matter. Tax rates change over time, as does your individual tax bracket. We will assume a marginal tax rate of 30 per cent plus a 2 per cent Medicare levy. This will be applied to a dividend yield of 4.17 per cent, which was the average yield of the ASX in 2024 according to S&P Dow Jones.

Income tax paid on dividends earned would be \$167 232 over the 20 years of our hypothetical scenario. This tax is not paid directly out of your portfolio; rather, it is paid separately when you file your tax. This is an issue that has caught many new investors off guard. To show the true impact on returns from taxes we subtracted the owed taxes from the value of the portfolio.

This also assumes that you don't face capital gains taxes that may be owed after selling any investment. Paying higher levels of capital gains tax is another impact of overtrading.

We can make assumptions on capital gains taxes at a high level. In this scenario the hypothetical investor contributed \$100 000 initially and \$1000 of additional investments every month for 20 years. This leads to a capital base of \$340 000. With the investment appreciating to \$1 317 062 the total capital gain would be \$977 062.

Assuming the portfolio holdings are retained for more than 12 months, a discount of 50 per cent is applied to capital gains taxes. At a 30 per cent marginal tax rate, the capital gains tax would \$156 330. However, some of the gains came from dividends and the tax was already paid. We used a dividend yield of a little more than 4 per cent, so we'll assume we owe only 60 per cent of the taxes for the capital gains, as 60 per cent of the returns came from the shares appreciating. That means a total tax of \$93 798.

The impact of poor behaviour

Behavioural impacts to returns stem from our tendency to make poor decisions in emotionally challenging investment environments. This is generally a reaction to volatility where the emotions of fear or greed are heighted. Investors tend to buy at the top of the market and sell at the bottom. Too many investors don't have an established strategy they can fall back on in times of stress.

We've cited several studies showing how poor timing decisions reduce the returns an investor achieves. This is called the 'behaviour gap' — the gap between an investment return and the return an investor earns. This is what is measured in Morningstar's 'Mind the Gap' study, which we discussed in earlier chapters. Constantly switching between different investments as an emotional response to volatility lowers returns for most investors.

We are going to apply the behavioural gap of 1.60 per cent that was found in the 'Mind the Gap' study in 2024. That gap means the average investor earned 1.60 per cent less per year than the total returns of the investments in their portfolio.

In our scenario the behavioural gap reduced the balance of the average investor by $277 210 over the 20-year period. And don't forget that poor behaviour would result in higher transaction costs and more taxes. These additional costs haven't been captured in our scenario.

Where do we end up?

There are many variables that can alter your outcomes. In this case the total nominal return of 10 per cent is reduced to 6 per cent per year from taxes, fees, transaction costs and poor behaviour. This is still a nominal return, as we haven't accounted for the impact of inflation, which further reduces the purchasing power of a portfolio. Taking into account the impact of taxes, transaction costs, fees, poor behaviour and inflation, a projected portfolio balance of \$1 391 009 was reduced to \$778 822. This is a significant difference.

The purpose of this exercise was to understand the different components of a total return and show that the figures widely quoted in the media can differ significantly from the returns an investor earns. We can clearly see that a 10 per cent headline return is not the return that investors will receive. This is particularly important to factor in when you are calculating what return you can reasonably expect to earn when setting your goals.

This exercise should be a wake-up call for investors. Minimising fees, taxes and transaction costs make a difference. Limiting poor behaviour and resisting the urge to churn a portfolio by constantly chasing the latest hot investments will make a difference. Headline returns are useful, but the return that is actually achieved is what matters.

How does this inform your edge as an investor?

The investment industrial complex spends a lot of time talking about returns while conveniently ignoring the impact of taxes, inflation and transaction fees on those returns. Fees are included in published returns of investment products but are ignored when looking at overall index returns.

The sales pitch for products that are not purely passive is often analytical edge. The investment industrial complex tells us that a star fund manager, a thematic or factor ETF, or rotating your portfolio will provide market-beating returns. This fosters an environment where investors believe they must constantly change their portfolio to capture this analytical edge. Yet to do this you give up the two sources of edge that anyone can achieve — behavioural and structural edge.

Following this path is the biggest impediment to achieving your goals. To achieve something different you must do something different from most investors. There are lots of different investment strategies you can use to achieve your goals. Yet the evidence is overwhelming that there is only one way to invest to do that. John Bogle was right to champion a strategy of minimising the impact of taxes, fees, transaction costs and poor behaviour. It doesn't matter whether you choose to take a purely passive approach, an active approach or a mix of both. What matters is that it is the best approach to help you achieve the outcome you want. When you make changes to your portfolio make sure it is based on your long-term strategy and not your short-term view of what the market will do. Make sure you are thinking about what you want out of life and how your portfolio will help you get there. In this book we've outlined the structure needed to create a personalised plan. It is up to you to follow your plan.

Exercise: Self-reflection

This is another exercise that may be challenging, but it should add perspective on the things that detract from returns. The goal of the exercise is to clarify how much you are paying in taxes, fees and transaction costs in a year. Pick a financial year and pull out your brokerage statements and tax records.

Start with taxes as this is the easiest one. How much tax did you pay on investment income and capital gains for the year?

(continued)

You can include any offsets from selling an investment at a loss and franking credits. Write down that number.

Next look at transaction fees. Multiply the number of times you traded last year by the brokerage cost for each transaction.

Finally look at fees. For any funds or ETFs you own, multiply the current value of each position by the annual management fee of that investment. Add up these values. If you pay any sort of admin fee include that as well. It may be a flat fee or expressed as a percentage; if a percentage multiply it by the current value of your portfolio.

Add the total of the fees, taxes and transaction costs together. Now take that number and divide it by the total value of your portfolio. The total is the percentage by which you are reducing your returns every year.

Go back to the required rate of return for your goal and see how that compares with what you are trying to earn to accomplish what you want out of life. Fees, taxes and transaction costs are inevitable, but there are ways to reduce them. Trade less and your transaction costs and taxes will be lower. Find lower cost funds and ETFs and your fees will be lower. What matters is what is left over in your account to spend. Focus on keeping as much of the returns you earn as possible.

On reducing taxes from longer holding periods

When we advocate for investors to delay paying taxes through longer holding periods, we often hear that taxes are simply a cost of success. Investors who don't fully understand compounding believe there is no difference between paying taxes this year or in five years. This isn't the case.

We've modelled a simple exercise to show the differences in timing around taxes. There are two scenarios in the exercise.

Scenario 1

In the first scenario we've assumed that an investment is held for one year and one day. That captures the capital gains discount for holding longer than a year. The investment is then sold, and a new investment is purchased.

That new investment is also held for one year and one day. The same process repeats over a five- and ten-year period. Each time one investment is sold and a new one is purchased, the amount invested is reduced by the taxes owed.

Scenario 2

In the second scenario the investment is held for the entire five- and ten-year period. It is then sold, and the applicable taxes are paid.

We've assumed the same return (10 per cent a year) in both scenarios. We've also assumed the investor stays in the same marginal tax bracket, but we've modelled the impact for an investor in the 45 per cent, 37 per cent and 30 per cent brackets.

Tables 8.1 and 8.2 (overleaf) show the results.

Table 8.1: 5-year return outcomes by marginal tax rate

Marginal tax rate (%)	Scenario 1: 5-year return with annual taxes (%)	Scenario 2: 5-year return taxes at end (%)
45	45.24	47.31
37	47.96	49.76
30	50.37	51.89

Table 8.2: 10-year return outcomes by marginal tax rate

Marginal tax rate (%)	Scenario 1: 10-year return with annual taxes (%)	Scenario 2: 10-year return taxes at end (%)
45	110.95	123.52
37	118.91	129.89
30	126.10	135.47

As you can see, holding the investment and paying the taxes later makes a difference. Many people are surprised by the result. This difference is the impact of breaking the chain of compounding. The longer the time period and the higher the taxes paid, the bigger the impact. Avoid anything that breaks the chain of compounding. There are more costs to trading too much than most investors understand.

Mark's view of success

Shani and I were struggling one day to come up with a topic for our weekly podcast. In fact, we were so desperate that Shani actually agreed to my idea of doing a podcast where we compared ourselves to a financial statement. The episode turned into a monologue of me comparing myself to a cash flow statement while Shani rolled her eyes and searched for a job that didn't involve listening to me.

Now she must read about the same topic in a book with her name on the cover. First, an explanation of the two financial statements in question. A balance sheet is a point-in-time snapshot of the assets and liabilities of a company. A cash flow statement looks at all the cash that comes in the door and all the cash that goes out the door. They are two parts of the financial statements that every company issues.

In Michael Lewis's book *Liar's Poker*, he talks about his experience on Wall Street. He recalled what the very wealthy traders thought 'rich' was. To them it was not a number. It was being able to afford the life they wanted on the income from US Treasury bonds. US Treasuries are considered risk free. What they were getting at is that if you could live the life you wanted to off interest from Treasuries, you were set for life. Nothing could ever threaten your lifestyle.

The capital base needed to get a comfortable income stream off risk-free bonds is significant, particularly when inflation is taken into account. This is not achievable for many of us, but the concept resonated with me and matched the way I saw investing.

We all live our lives on a cash flow basis. We have a job and periodically get paid a certain amount, which we use to pay for our life. My goal is to create passive income and have my investments pay me an income instead of having to work for it. In other words, I'm worried about my personal cash flow statement. How much money is coming in the door and how much is going out. When I judge my success as an investor I'm focused on how my investments contribute to my cash flow statement.

Then there is the balance sheet approach to life. This is more in line with how people define traditional financial success. Being 'rich' is often thought of as a number. Your net worth is how you judge your success, but it is always changing. If you invest in the stock market, your net worth will go up and down every day. There can be profound changes in your net worth over the course of a relatively short timeframe, but does anything about your lifestyle change?

(continued)

I like this quote from television series *The Wire*: 'You only spend two days in gaol: the day you go in and the day you get out.' Investing is similar. If you are speculating, or simply counting price appreciation, there are only two prices that matter: the price when you buy and the price when you sell. The fluctuations in between have no impact on your life.

I want to focus on what happens in between the purchase and the sale, because I'm living my life during that period, and I want it to be better. This is why I focus on cash flow. This is cash flow produced by companies and returned as dividends. An obsession with net worth is counterproductive to this focus.

This leads to my unconventional view on housing. From the perspective of a balance sheet, someone might look wealthy when they buy a home. They have a huge asset on their balance sheet with a large amount of debt tied to it. They go into a ton of debt and their mortgage payment makes up a large portion of their income. After years of sacrificing and self-denial as they save for a house, now they can't do fun things because they own a house. People continue to do this because housing prices go up, and suddenly house owners are considered wealthy because their net worth rises. In a world focused on balance sheets it makes sense to stretch for a house.

The only way they could get cash flow from this asset would be to take out another loan, or sell the house and move into something smaller or in a cheaper location. This pursuit of balance sheet wealth creates a cycle. People keep trading up in houses and keep taking on more debt. In my opinion, this approach makes people less financially secure and more dependent on their jobs as they get older, instead of giving them freedom and more choices.

Another advantage of the cash flow approach is behavioural. The obsession with net worth can drive really poor decision making. When the market is going up, and you hear about how all these speculative investments are earning huge returns, you are more inclined to chase them because you have a short-term focus on your net worth. When the market is falling, and you are fixated on your net worth, you are more likely to sell. My focus on cash flow and income means that when the market goes down there is more opportunity to earn income.

This is because of how dividend yield works. To calculate the yield, you divide the dividend by the price of the share. As long as the dividend is maintained, if the price goes down you will earn more income off the money you invest.

There are many different approaches to investing that work. But what is guaranteed *not* to work is not understanding the decisions you are making and what factors lead to success in your approach. If you are cash flow inclined, what matters is the sustainability of those cash flows and your ability to get to a level where those cash flows can support you. If you are more focused on your balance sheet, you need to be cognisant of the risks you are taking when you take on debt. And you need to be clear about how you are going to convert your assets into cash to pay for your life. This can be problematic when asset prices are going down.

Shani's definition of success

One measure of success I like to focus on is my own behaviour. A common theme I always highlight is my focus on controlling what I can control.

(continued)

In the past few years I've had career and salary growth. My focus is ensuring that I recognise this growth as an opportunity to further secure my financial goals. Every pay rise I get is an opportunity to contribute more to my investment accounts. It's an opportunity to pay down my mortgage.

At the start of every year I look at both the performance of my investments and how much I've saved. Saving is within my control. My savings levels reflect how much I contribute to my goals, which stems from my ability to prevent lifestyle creep and keep my financial goals front of mind. My investment performance is a measure of markets that are out of my control. I always keep in mind that volatility does not impact me over the long term.

I like to constantly remind myself that success doesn't always have to be performance based. There are many factors within my control that can increase my chances of success.

I understand that there will be a time in my career that my savings levels will no longer be on an upward trajectory. It will naturally flatten out, and that's okay. I just want to ensure that lifestyle creep does not impact my long-term goals, and I'm thoughtful about what I save and spend.

Key takeaways

Behavioural and structural edge are the two sources of competitive advantage that all investors can take advantage of. The key to achieving this edge is education and structured decision making. The only returns that matter are the ones you get to keep, which means taxes, fees and inflation need to be considered along with the impact of your own mistakes. Always focus on minimising anything that takes away from your returns.

The exercise in this chapter was more about self-reflection than a building block for your personalised financial strategy. This should bring home the impact of taxes, fees and transaction costs. Keep this in mind as you continue to design your plan for financial independence.

Create your investment strategy

Mike Tyson famously said that everyone has a plan until they get hit in the face. He also lost a $400 million fortune and went bankrupt. We will use his words as inspiration but take financial advice from people who didn't blow their fortune on jewellery, limousines and tigers!

For investors the proverbial punch in the face is market downturns, and most people take that punch without having a plan to fall back on. At this point you know more about yourself and what you want to accomplish than most people. You've set yourself up for success. Now it's time to come up with your own personalised plan, and this will involve an investment strategy.

You have completed the foundational steps of successful investing by shaping your money philosophy and establishing your investment goals. You've thought about diversification as it relates to your goals. You've explored what might detract from your returns. You know a bit more about compounding and you've reframed the way the investment industry thinks about risk. You can now focus on the life you want.

Completing your plan with an investment strategy will enable you to avoid being distracted by all the noise coming from changes in markets and the constant commentary from market 'experts'. People without a plan struggle to evaluate how they are progressing because they have no context in which to judge performance.

An Investment Policy Statement is a set of rules that governs how professional investors operate. It outlines what they can and can't invest in and acts as a contract between the people who put up the money and the people investing it on their behalf. We will use the same principle in creating your investment strategy, though in this case the 'contract' will be with yourself.

Your investment strategy will outline what you're investing in and why. It will connect your investments with the goal you are trying to achieve. You will have more confidence in the investments you hold once you know they are connected to your goal.

Your investment strategy will include your asset allocation target, your criteria for selecting securities and the process by which you will maintain your portfolio. It will guide you through making important decisions such as when you will buy and sell investments and how often you will rebalance your portfolio. It will help prevent poor behaviour. Following a strategy leads to better outcomes than constantly acting on a whim.

There are many benefits to this approach. As we've stressed, setting down a plan makes it more likely you will accomplish it. If you will forgive a brief and completely unqualified foray into neuroscience, there are two benefits to writing things down: external memory and encoding. External memory in this case is simply the visual cue, the memory aid that is your written plan. Encoding is the process by which your brain chooses to remember some things and discard others. Writing down your plan enhances the likelihood you will remember it, and accomplish your goal.

Your investment strategy will build on the structure of your goal-setting process. We'll return to Morningstar's 'Mind the Gap' study for evidence of how this helps investors. You will recall that the study distinguished between investor and investment returns, with investors substantially underperforming their investments due to poor timing decisions.

Morningstar examined the case of target allocation funds in which a set asset allocation is maintained by periodic rebalancing. This is a set-and-forget one-stop fund, similar to a pre-mixed option offered by many of the large industry super funds.

In the study, target allocation funds were compared to narrower funds in which investors are more likely to trade. The research found the mechanised nature of maintaining target allocation funds helped investors avoid the costs of trying to time the market. The gap between investor and investment returns disappeared.

Investors in these funds are generally not trying to time the market. They are largely set-and-forget, and by doing nothing they earn higher returns than those investors who try to deftly navigate the market. The goal of creating a personalised investment strategy that is aligned with your goal is to achieve the same thing.

Shani says...

When people think about investment strategies, their minds usually jump to complex logic and criteria, but your strategy doesn't need to be complicated to succeed. The simpler it is, the more likely it is to succeed. The key to a successful investment strategy is not picking the best investments so much as forming the clearest line between what you need to achieve your goals and how the investments you pick relate to those factors. This will give you the best chance of reaching your financial goals.

Now to the process of creating an investment strategy. You needn't complete this exercise in one sitting. Not only are there are lots of things to think about, but your investment strategy is a living, breathing document that you will review and refine periodically as you gain experience and knowledge.

Step 1: Define your overall approach

This step turns achieving your goals into a high-level investment approach. In setting your goals you have specified the outcome you want to achieve. For instance, you may want a portfolio that is worth $100k in 10 years or you may have a goal of generating income of $20k a year in 10 years. As part of the goal-definition process, you've estimated what it takes to achieve that from both a returns perspective and from a savings perspective.

Your investment approach should reflect the type of portfolio required to achieve your specific goal. There's no need to write *War and Peace* here. If your goal is to earn 8 per cent a year and save $100k in 10 years, your investment approach could be simply to invest in growth assets to achieve capital growth with a 10-year time horizon.

Clarity is key. Quantifying and prioritising your goals is paramount. If you don't quantify your goals, you can't measure success. If you don't prioritise your goals, there's a risk your lack of focus will hinder you from achieving any of your goals. You will layer more details into the investment strategy in the future. The investment approach lays the foundation for the entire strategy.

Step 2: Set your asset allocation

Studies have shown that asset allocation is the single largest driver of long-term returns. Later in this chapter Shani goes into some detail on asset allocation in her investment strategy, but for now it's sufficient to say this is the most important step an investor can take. At a high level, your asset allocation will be spread between growth and defensive assets.

In theory, and historically, growth assets such as shares have higher returns than defensive assets like cash or bonds. This means if a higher return is needed to meet an investment goal, a larger portion of a portfolio will need to be allocated to growth assets. Simple as that.

Asset allocation gets more complex as you drill down. For example, some investors are making decisions on how much to allocate to emerging market equities versus small cap equities. We have nothing against this approach. However, it's worth noting that the largest driver of a portfolio's future expected returns comes from the high-level decision made in allocating to growth and defensive assets. If you are comfortable stopping at that level, things will be just fine.

Complexity brings benefits but there are also downsides. As we've noted, monitoring a complex portfolio demands time as well as more rebalancing, which has tax implications. We're not saying don't do this. Just be mindful of the implications.

We'll return to diversification but for now remember that it's not the same thing as asset allocation. Asset allocation is about designing a portfolio to achieve a specific goal based on return and volatility objectives. The purpose of diversification is to remove single-security, sector and asset-class risk from a portfolio.

Remember to focus on your risk capacity or how much risk you will need to take to achieve your goal.

Assets move in value as prices changes. It may be best to aim for a range for your asset allocation. For example, you might have an 80 per cent allocation to equities, but on any given day that 80 per cent could make up from 75 to 85 per cent of your portfolio. For that reason, value your equities asset allocation as 75 to 85 per cent rather than 80 per cent.

We covered historical returns in chapter 1, but you can also look at likely future returns. Morningstar Investment Management projects returns on a variety of asset classes into the future. Table 9.1 shows those projections.

Table 9.1: projected returns by asset class

Asset class	Projected return over the next 20 years (%)
Australian shares	7.90
International shares	6.75
Australian listed property	6.85
International listed property	7.00
Australian fixed interest	2.00
International fixed interest	2.25
Cash	1.75

Source: Morningstar data

Remember that you need to set an asset allocation that has a reasonable chance of achieving the return you need for your goal over the long term. No-one has a crystal ball, but the combination of Morningstar's projections and historic returns for different assets can provide you with reasonable guidance on asset allocation.

Step 3: Determine your edge

The foundation of your investment strategy is now all but in place. The approach and asset-allocation target will guide the criteria for selection. One important step remains to be completed.

We've explained the different sources of investor edge, and you've already begun to think about the competitive advantage you have as an investor that will help you achieve each of your goals. Now identify and write down the sources of edge you believe you have, why you think you have that edge and what you need to do to take advantage of it. Don't worry if you've read through the list of sources of edge and none seem to apply to you. It might be best just to invest passively. Buying an index fund or ETF and regularly contributing to your portfolio is a great way to build long-term wealth. The key here is consistency. If the market goes up or it goes down continue to invest in regular intervals (dollar-cost average). Just stick to your plan. If you don't have a source of edge, the less you do the better.

Mark says...

People underestimate the benefit of writing down a strategy. Writing anything down forces you to think and clarifies what may be holding you back. It removes anxiety and simplifies the thoughts that are bouncing through your mind. Perhaps most importantly, it enables you to refer to your strategy when you're stressed and markets are turbulent. That alone can keep you from making countless mistakes.

Step 4: Identify your security selection criteria

There are thousands of publicly listed shares, funds and ETFs. This abundance of choice can be challenging, especially when there are so many articulate advocates of different investment strategies and products. Remember that their goals and yours may not be aligned.

Ironically people's varying reactions to this confusing environment have little to do with their experience or knowledge. Those who are new to investing may feel overwhelmed by the seeming complexity of investment options. Experienced investors can feel equally overwhelmed by the potential flaws they can see in each option. Both sets of investors may suffer from analysis paralysis.

Investors who make the leap and buy may soon suffer buyer's remorse and be tempted by alternate choices. This temptation is exacerbated by the fear of missing out when faced with constant commentary on the merits of different strategies, markets and individual securities. Short-term price movements are also challenging as recency bias can cause many investors to assume that — good or bad — current trends will persist. This all contributes to the constant churning of investor portfolios.

To cut through the dizzying array of options it helps to use set criteria when selecting investments. Defining your security selection criteria narrows the field and creates a more concentrated list of options. You can instantly eliminate an investment that isn't aligned to your goals or investment strategy. It also lessens the temptation to change investment approaches by maintaining the connection between a goal-aligned investment strategy and portfolio holdings.

Your goal is to create a simple set of guidelines to follow when picking an investment. We don't think you can rely on your willpower alone or any absorbed market folklore to continually make good decisions over decades. These guidelines will give you a place to turn to when you are stressed by a market drop and a brake on FOMO when markets are soaring.

A decision tree for security selection can simplify the process of selecting from an abundance of choice (figure 9.1).

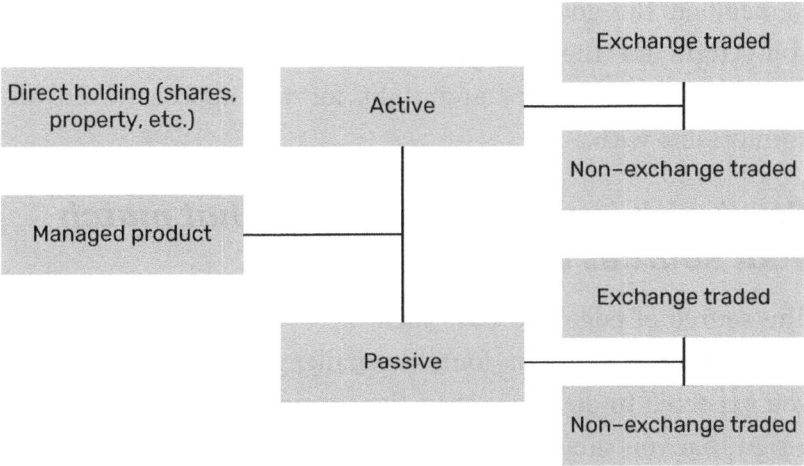

Figure 9.1: decision tree for security selection

You may have different security selection criteria for different asset classes you want exposure to. This can be based on several factors. For example, an investor may want to invest in individual Australian companies because they are familiar with the local market and because of the ease of trading. For emerging markets, the same investor may want to use an ETF or fund because the markets are less familiar and because it is very difficult to buy direct shares.

For new investors this step may be challenging. It takes time and knowledge but also, most importantly, clear thinking to align a goal to the selection criteria. We suggest you get something on paper and refine it over time as you gain experience and clarify your thoughts.

We also suggest you don't invest in anything you don't understand. If you can't figure out why a specific type of investment will help you achieve your goal, exclude it. There's nothing wrong with a simple portfolio with just a few passive ETFs. Simplicity, as we've reiterated, can give you a real advantage.

Remember, the goal is to find investments that are right for you — right for the goal you want to achieve, right for your personal circumstances and right for the approach you are comfortable with.

Start with investment vehicles that match your sources of edge

The source of edge you have identified will play a role in your investing criteria. If you found it challenging to articulate how you expected to do better than the average investor, it might be a sign that you should either get some help with managing your portfolio or stick to passive investing.

NO EDGE

This is the first step of the selecting investments decision tree. No edge means no individual shares and no thematic or factor ETFs. You'll get exposure to the market — or to that part of the market that aligns with the return you need to achieve your goal and earn the average or index return. There's no shame in this approach. Focus on saving money and let the index do its job. This is a very effective approach to building wealth.

INFORMATIONAL OR ANALYTICAL EDGE

If you believe you have informational and analytical edge, it's worth considering where this plays out. Will it allow you to pick the companies that will best enable you to achieve your goals? If so, your focus should be on purchasing individual shares.

Do you believe your informational and analytical edge allows you to identify undervalued asset classes or pockets of the market? If so, your investment universe opens up to individual shares and index-tracking funds or ETFs. The key is to direct funds into attractive opportunities and avoid unattractive parts of the market.

Do you believe you can pick the right managers who will enable you to achieve your goal? If so, you will seek out active funds and ETFs with talented managers.

But as we've said, it's extremely difficult for any investor to maintain long-term informational and analytical edge.

BEHAVIOURAL OR STRUCTURAL EDGE

If you believe you have behavioural or structural edge, the key is discipline. You can choose any type of investment, but making good decisions is paramount. The process of defining an investment strategy is critical to success, as it applies structure to enable rational assessments of opportunities while eliminating or minimising emotional reactions to volatility. Once you have a well-defined strategy, you just need to follow it. Sometimes that may be easier said than done, but not having a strategy guarantees you won't be successful.

Shani chooses to invest in managed funds and ETFs because she believes her competitive advantage in achieving her goals is not her competitive advantage in selecting individual investments. Mark's view is that he has a structural and behavioural edge related to achieving his goal of generating income. He picks individual shares and ETFs but holds them over the long term because he doesn't think he can consistently navigate markets better than other investors.

Your personal circumstances: tax

Personal circumstances play a role in which investments you choose. Your goal should be to minimise the impact of taxes on your returns, but how much this matters is a function of the tax environment.

If you are a super investor in the pension phase, taxes can be ignored. If you're in a lower marginal tax bracket or in super during the accumulation phase, you should be moderately concerned with minimising taxes. If you're investing money outside of super in high marginal tax brackets, minimising taxes is paramount.

Remember, your behaviour will have a large influence on the returns you'll achieve. The more you trade, the more taxes you'll pay. If you are selling investments that you've held for less than a year, you won't benefit from the long-term discount on capital gains. We cover this in step 5.

The type of investment also matters. Both ETFs and funds distribute capital gains to investors when they occur. In general, an actively managed ETF or fund will generate more capital gains than passive products. Some thematic or factor ETFs have a high turnover due to rebalancing, and this too will have tax consequences. It's important to understand how this works.

The advantage of holding individual shares is that you get to choose when capital gains are realised. If you don't sell, you won't pay capital gains taxes.

Your personal circumstances: transaction costs

Transaction costs vary depending on your broker. And as we've already discussed, they are also impacted by your behaviour. Fewer trades means lower transaction costs. Transaction costs also consist of buy/sell spreads. Many investors don't consider this to be a cost, but costs can build up over time if you trade too much.

If you are saving and investing regularly with a high-cost broker, transaction costs may play a role in the type of investment you choose. Funds do not have transaction costs, and the savings plans that many managed funds provide may have lower investment limits.

This is the way Shani invests. With every pay cheque, she contributes to managed funds and ETFs. Because these funds do not incur brokerage or transaction costs, she is able to avoid the fees that would be detrimental to her total returns over the long term.

Don't get caught up in the hype of a narrative about a certain type of investment. Different types of investments will suit different types of investors. They are all simply a means to an end. Table 9.2 (overleaf) lists some of the broad cost differences that can guide your thinking.

Write down which types of investment you will consider as part of your investment strategy.

Table 9.2: high-level comparison of investment products

	Equities	**Funds**	**ETFs**	**Listed investment companies (LICs)**
Transaction cost	Standard brokerage	None	Standard brokerage	Standard brokerage
Management fee	None	Generally slightly more	Generally slightly less	Generally slightly more
Trading flexibility	Higher	Lower	Higher	Higher
Minimum investment	Depends on stock price	Generally higher	Lower	Lower
Behavioural risk	Higher	Lower	Higher	Higher

Active or passive?

If you have chosen collective investment vehicles such as funds or ETFs, there's another branch of the decision tree to consider. It concerns one of the questions we are asked most often: should I be an active or passive investor? There is no obvious champion. The answer will depend on your individual goals and circumstances.

Morningstar conducts a semi-annual report called the 'Active Passive Barometer' that compares the relative success of active and passive approaches. Although the data is based on the US market, Australian investors can glean valuable insights based on the similar characteristics of the two markets.

This study is conducted biannually, and the results are largely consistent. It reveals how difficult it is for active managers to beat passive managers over the long term. Investing is a highly competitive endeavour and, not surprisingly, active managers charge higher fees than their passive counterparts, which detracts from returns. The mid-year 2024 'Active Passive Barometer' report shows that only 28 per cent of active managers beat their passive counterparts over a 10-year period. As we've said, it's hard to beat an index.

However, the success rate of active management varies across different asset classes. Active management typically works better in markets whose investors pay less attention or where a broader index allows good active managers to differentiate their portfolio from the index.

Two examples are real estate and bonds. In both of these asset classes, active managers have tended to do better than their passive peers over the long term (table 9.3). What we can also see from the table below is that fees matter. Given that fees for active funds with an above-average success rate are most often in the lowest-cost quintile, fees are key for investors looking to invest in most managed funds or ETF products.

Table 9.3: active funds' success rate by category

Category	10-year (lowest cost) (%)*	10-year (highest cost) (%)
US Large Blend	19.7	6.8
US Large Value	20.3	18.5
US Large Growth	27.5	18.2
US Mid Blend	18.2	4.3
US Mid Value	26.3	31.8
US Mid Growth	33.3	27.9
US Small Blend	33.3	36.8
US Small Value	38.1	45.5
US Small Growth	42.9	41.9

(continued)

Table 9.3: *(continued)*

Category	10-year (lowest cost) (%)*	10-year (highest cost) (%)
Foreign Large Blend	45.5	17.1
Foreign Large Value	41.2	30.0
Foreign Small/Mid Blend	40.0	16.7
Global Large Blend	0	16.7
Diversified Emerging Markets	37.8	27.0
Europe Stock	25.0	40.0
US Real Estate	53.8	42.9
Global Real Estate	44.4	36.4
Intermediate Core Bond	52.2	25.9
Corporate Bond	57.1	60.0
High-Yield Bond	38.7	24.3

Source: Morningstar. Data and calculations as of June 30, 2024.
*The shading indicates that active funds in this quintile had above-average success rates.

Defining investment criteria

By now you should have defined the types of investments you will consider. For instance, you might have concluded that you will only invest using ETFs. Or perhaps you've decided you will invest in multiple types of investments, including shares and ETFs. This is a good first step. Now you need criteria for selecting the individual holdings. For example, if you are investing in ETFs you need to figure out how you will pick which ETFs should be in your portfolio.

The criteria you define may be very complicated or very simple. It all depends on what you are trying to accomplish and your own investing skill and knowledge. A passive investor might simply buy the index ETFs with the lowest fees. If you are buying individual shares your selection criteria might be extensive.

This book is not primarily about picking investments. It is about the process you will follow in order to achieve your goals. In the next chapter we share some thoughts on where investors can go wrong with different types of investments. And because we have very different approaches, later in this chapter, we will outline our personal strategies to help show the range of criteria for choosing a particular asset class or share.

More than anything your ability to define your selection criteria will be a window into which investments you should consider. As we've argued, if you can't articulate why you would buy one share over another, we don't think you should be buying shares. The same goes for thematic or factor ETFs. If you don't know how to choose one over the other, just choose to invest passively.

Write out the criteria you will use to select securities. Think about why meeting these criteria will increase the likelihood that the investment you select will contribute to meeting your long-term goals.

Step 5: Establish the basis for making changes to your portfolio

Your investment strategy is a framework for making investment decisions that will ensure alignment with your goal. The point is to minimise mistakes.

The genesis of investment mistakes is the failure to understand what you are trying to accomplish and how to achieve a specific goal. The manifestation of those mistakes is purchasing the wrong investments in the first place and constantly switching holdings in a portfolio.

Setting criteria for making changes to a portfolio provides structure to making rational decisions around portfolio turnover.

Three broad categories drive changes to a portfolio:

1. rebalancing
2. an investment no longer meets the original thesis
3. a change in your circumstances.

Before we walk through each of these categories, let's consider a trap many investors fall into, which is the main cause of chronic overtrading. It's the suspicion that there may be a better opportunity than a current holding.

On the surface this rationale seems logical. If an investor believes that in the future an investment will outperform one they already hold, logic dictates it should be purchased with the proceeds from the sale of a current holding. When tempted to make such a trade it is worth thinking long and hard about its merits.

Many investors succumb to recency bias and simply extrapolate the short-term outperformance of the new investment opportunity into the future. Ask yourself whether recency bias is shaping your thinking. Or perhaps you have simply been seduced by a compelling narrative. Investors have long chased performance for similar reasons and the outcomes are often poor.

Let's turn back to Ben Graham. In *The Intelligent Investor*, Graham captured the folly of the approach that many investors take in his parable of Mr Market. Many investors are overly fixated on price changes and think short-term movements better reveal the merits of an investment than they actually do. This makes it easy to conflate price with value. Short-term price movements are often divorced from the long-term prospects of a company. They are emotional reactions to new data that will be inconsequential over the long run. Whether you are focused on behavioural and/or structural edge or are taking a passive approach, it makes no sense to follow the herd.

If you are focused on informational or analytical edge, it is worth remembering that what matters is after-tax outcomes and that transaction fees and taxes detract from returns. That means that just to break even the return on a new investment must exceed that of the one that was sold by the transaction costs and taxes. This means most of the time the new investment has to perform significantly better than the one you sold for it to impact your overall outcome positively.

There is also the risk that you may be wrong in your assessment of the relative merits of the two investments. As we have previously pointed out, Morningstar's annual 'Mind the Gap' study shows annual investor returns to be 1.60 per cent lower than the actual returns of the underlying investments. That shortfall is based on poor timing decisions — in other words, on investors trading because they have incorrectly judged the relative merits of two investments.

'Mind the Gap' is far from the only study showing the downside of frequent trading. Researchers Brad Barber and Terrance Odean concluded in their article 'Trading Is Hazardous to Your Wealth' that between 1991 and 1996 individual investors who traded most earned an annual return 6.5 per cent lower than that earned by the overall sharemarket.

Following are the most significant reasons to make changes to a portfolio.

Rebalancing

There are times when a portfolio needs to be adjusted. For example, if the allocation to an asset class grows or shrinks it may no longer align with your asset allocation target. Large differences can make it harder to achieve your goals. The same applies if a single position becomes too large. If that position were to fall significantly, it could prevent you from achieving your goal.

We documented our asset allocation target in step 2 of the strategy. Now we need to decide how large a single position can be allowed to be before a change becomes necessary. Having already begun to think about this as you completed the exercise in which you defined your investment strategy, you will have a general feeling about what to choose.

Remember, the point of diversification is to reduce security-specific risk in a portfolio in case something goes wrong with a particular company you own. How much you diversify away that security-specific risk is up to you.

Write down the conditions under which you would rebalance your portfolio. It may be when your overall asset allocation to a particular asset class is plus or minus 5 per cent from your target. It may be when a single share grows to be worth more than 5 per cent of your portfolio. In establishing your rules, remember that selling often has consequences in transaction costs and taxes. We both try not to sell if we can help it and try to adjust in other ways, such as directing new savings away from the overrepresented asset class or position. But sometimes there is no choice but to rebalance.

An investment no longer meets the original thesis

In step 4 of the strategy you outlined the selection criteria for picking individual holdings for a portfolio. The reasons why a particular holding meets those criteria is your thesis. Investing is not black and white and judgement calls need to be made.

Even if past financial metrics are being used as inputs into your decision making, your assumption could be that certain trends will continue or they will reverse.

The purpose of defining a strategy is to ensure that every investment you pick meets a set of criteria at the time of purchase, but things — conditions, companies — can change. This occurs far less frequently than is popularly portrayed, but it does happen. There will be investments in your portfolio that don't work. That's just life. Remember, that is the reason you diversify. Not everything you buy will be a winner. You just need to get more right than wrong — or a couple very right.

Before deciding to replace a holding, remember to never sell a company just because it's going through a rough patch, and never buy based on a single good quarter or year. Patience is key.

Examples of changes in circumstances around an investment range from an increase in fees on an ETF to a fundamental change in a company. We recommend you document the reason for choosing every investment. After establishing your selection criteria this shouldn't be hard. Just set out why the investment will continue to meet your criteria and how that will lead to a good outcome.

Once you have written down why you've bought a particular investment it's simple to go back and refer to your original criteria to see whether circumstances have changed. Many investors can't remember why something ended up in their portfolio, perhaps because they had no good reason to buy in the first place. Coming up with set criteria and recognising why an investment meets those criteria mean you won't be that investor.

Investor circumstances change

Over time your circumstances will inevitably change, perhaps as you approach a goal or as a result of the natural process of ageing. This may be a time to reconsider the holdings in your portfolio. The best thing to do is to go back to the beginning and refine your strategy so each part remains aligned. Then you can evaluate each investment against your new criteria.

Bringing it all together

Defining your investment strategy takes a bit of work, and the next exercise is one of the longest in the book. It will involve some serious thought, and again you don't have to complete the exercise in one sitting.

If you've gone through each step in this chapter, think about what you've accomplished. You now know which types of investments you'll consider and which you'll ignore. You have an asset allocation target that is designed to help you achieve your goals. You've defined your selection criteria and the conditions under which you will make changes to your portfolio.

This is an amazing accomplishment. You've set yourself up for success. You should be very proud of completing a step most people never take. You are now truly on the pathway to financial freedom.

Shani's investment strategy

Each of my financial goals has a different time horizon and requires a different risk capacity so different assets are tied to them. However, getting to know myself as an investor has meant that I understand what works for me and the best way to maximise the success of my portfolio.

This is investing my way. It's investing in the way that serves my needs, which will be different from your needs. There are some investments I steer clear of, yet these same investments make up the majority of Mark's portfolio. Our goals are different. We are different people. Investments are a means to an end. I choose to focus on other drivers of portfolio returns that will contribute most to reaching my financial goals over the long term.

For me, the start is constructing solid foundations for my financial plan. Many investors chase the highs of bull markets and are happy to pile in money during the ascent. It is natural and common to falter when volatility strikes.

Studies have shown time and time again that volatility shakes investors who do not have a solid foundation in place and leads to panic and poor decision making. This is especially true if investors are holding securities that they chose because they promised quick wins. Conviction is only skin deep if you buy an investment because you think it will only go up. That conviction evaporates quickly during a downturn.

Like many people, I took the leap into investing before figuring out what I was trying to accomplish. As I developed my goals and my savings plan, I started reflecting on my investment strategy. Most investors believe that investment success requires constantly finding the best investments. I was one of those investors for a long time. The foundation of this belief is that at any particular moment there are good investments that will outperform in the immediate future and bad investments that will underperform. This view is reinforced and encouraged by professional investors who are selling their ability to navigate markets in their search for opportunities.

(continued)

I've learned that investment success isn't about finding the best-performing securities but about building a sustainable, goal-oriented strategy. My approach prioritises asset allocation and saving money rather than stock-picking. This suits my temperament and my view that I do not have an investing edge that I can leverage. Outsourcing my investment decisions will result in the best outcomes for me.

I've come to my approach for technical and circumstantial reasons. Let's start with the technical. In their seminal paper from 1986, 'Determinants of Portfolio Performance', Gary Brinson, Randolph Hood and Gilbert Beebower attributed 93.6 per cent of investment performance to asset allocation. The paper focused not on the return level but on the variation of returns. A 1991 update concluded active decisions on investment selection by pension plans (the basis for the study) made little improvement to performance over a 10-year period. The paper championed a focus on strategic asset allocation over the long term to increase the chances of reaching successful outcomes.

There were several adaptations of this research by other academics, including Roger Ibbotson and Paul Kaplan's 2000 report 'Does Asset Allocation Explain 40, 90 or 100 Percent of Performance?'. Ibbotson and Kaplan focused on a key question for investors — what percentage of actual returns come from the asset allocation decisions they make? Ibbotson explains the results in a 2010 CFA Institute paper ('The Importance of Asset Allocation') with the following logic:

- Asset allocation policy gives us the passive return (beta). The rest of the return can be attributed to active return (alpha).
- The alpha is zero (before costs) because on average, active managers do not outperform the market.

- As a result, passive asset allocation determines 100 per cent of the return before costs, and more than 100 per cent of the return after costs.

Ibbotson's point is that because most investors can't put together a portfolio of individual investments that beats the index, the only driver of returns is the asset allocation of their overall portfolios.

The second guiding principle to my investing strategy is a focus on factors within my control as I try to build wealth and achieve my goals. I save by minimising taxes and fees and limiting the impact of poor decisions on my investment approach. I have rigid savings goals that are governed by my investment strategy. I try to consider these as non-negotiable fixed costs.

I haven't read any academic papers on the importance of saving. I don't think any academic is going to get accolades for pointing out the revolutionary idea that capital is important to build wealth. The maths isn't difficult. If I plan to contribute $1000 a month but am able to contribute $100 extra, it is as though I have achieved the equivalent of a 10 per cent monthly return. Of course, there's an opportunity cost attached to extra contributions — you don't get to spend the money. You don't have this same cost with actual investment returns. I'll come back to touch on my experiences with savings and how they have formed such an integral part of my perception of successful investing.

Academic arguments are interesting, but they often ignore the realities of life. Nassim Taleb writes about this in his book *Skin in the Game*. For him, 'skin in the game' is a metaphor for the contact with the real world that informs your decision making: 'The knowledge we get by tinkering, via trial and error, experience and the workings of time…is vastly superior to that obtained through reasoning.'

(continued)

He refers to *Pathemata mathemata*, a Greek concept that refers to how abrasions on your skin guide your learning – or, in other words, learning through experience. Investing has not drawn actual blood (yet), but I strongly believe that your circumstances, temperament and direct experiences guide the type of investor you are and the investing strategy that will maximise your outcomes.

Two groups prioritise security selection – investors and speculators. New investors tend to attack security selection first, as strong returns are often an inducement to get into the market. We saw this with the influx of new investors in 2020 and 2021. These investors rode the wave of COVID market returns and became prematurely confident of their investment selection capabilities. They experienced a momentum-fuelled rally that meant buying shares paid off. I would classify a large cohort of these new entrants as speculators who made tactical allocations based on recent performance.

This was a perfect example of riding the asset-class wave and mistakenly attributing it to individual prowess. Since then, despite volatility, markets have continued to climb to new highs, but a contraction, and consequently a reality check, is inevitable. Historically, we've had a bear market every 3.5 years, and it's folly to think we will avoid one in the near future.

You're more likely to stick to your investment strategy if you understand how the investments you hold connect to your financial goals. This understanding will make it less likely that you sell at inopportune moments to try to time the market. If you only have surface-level faith in an asset, you're more likely to sell it in times of volatility.

It's also worth mentioning that in bear markets the tactical allocation of funds can severely rig the game against you. Over the past 30 years, if you had missed the S&P 500's

10 best days, your return would have been cut in half. If you had missed the best 30 days over the past 30 years, your return would have been 83 per cent lower.

This is why timing the market is an issue but also why an overreliance on tactical asset allocation in your investment strategy can also be an issue. Not being invested in the right securities means missing most of those days. Seventy-eight per cent of the best days occurred in a bear market. I don't want to miss out. I am perfectly content to capture the average return of the market.

Just as bull markets drive new investors, bear markets cause people to give up. Those who don't quit may find their way to adopting a strategy that focuses more on what they are trying to achieve, rather than the vehicles that will get them there.

My portfolio today

Fast forward to today. My portfolio outside of superannuation consists of cash and collective investment vehicles—managed funds and ETFs. These are mostly broad indexes that are passively managed. The investment vehicles are concentrated mainly in equities. My cash is held in my emergency fund. Mark and I hate investment or investor labels, but if I were to choose a label for myself, it would be 'passive investor'.

I no longer feel the need to justify my investment decisions at every turn of the market. My portfolio is connected to a solid foundation—my goals. I have a strong understanding of why I hold each position and why it behaves the way it does through different market conditions. This understanding means that I am not tempted by each new opportunity. I have a long time horizon during which my capital will grow and compound. I've evolved my perception of investing from maximising wealth to building a model that works best to maximise my outcomes (figure 9.2, overleaf).

(continued)

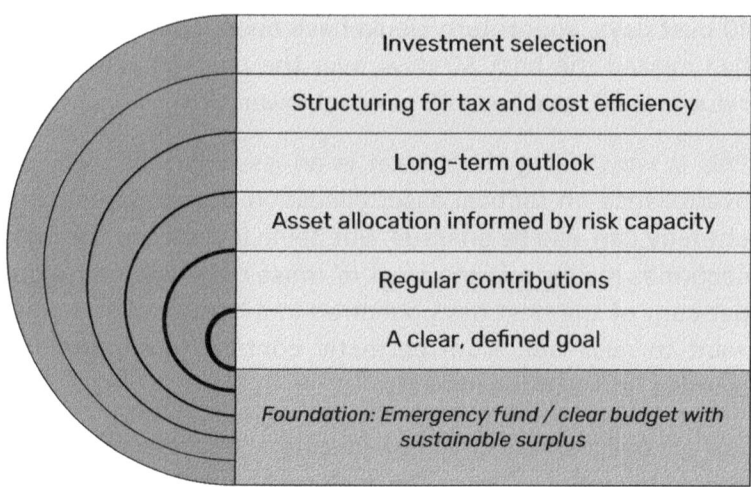

Figure 9.2: a model to maximise Shani's outcomes

This has had a flow-on effect to other benefits. I am more tax efficient. I limit selling and that lowers my transaction costs (as well as tax). I am cost-conscious. I stay invested for the long term. I think about how to structure my investments so they are in the most tax-efficient vehicle. These benefits are hugely important when considering total return outcomes. In chapter 8, this was outlined in the reduction of returns from the hypothetical 10 per cent.

This is why it's important to me that I'm able to focus on the factors within my control. It leads to better outcomes for me than if I were making direct equity decisions.

This brings me back to one of the main factors I can control: savings. The importance of saving was one of the lessons I learned when coming up with my wealth-building blueprint when I worked for the asset manager. Investing at regular intervals regardless of what the market is doing will lead to successful outcomes over the long term. The market has always trended upwards over the long term. Saving with discipline, and without trying to time the market, led to success in the account histories I reviewed as part of my job.

Selecting investments brings a lot of people joy. My investment strategy does not discredit this approach. Mark enjoys the intellectual challenge of active investing and choosing direct equities suits his temperament. The lesson is that each investor is different, and a blanket approach is not going to work. I am much more focused on investing regularly in the right asset allocation and committing over the long term. I believe that will provide more of a difference to my outcome than choosing between stocks.

What Mark and I have in common is an intrinsic understanding of ourselves and our goals. The simplicity we bring to our investment decisions and our portfolios is the cornerstone of our success.

Now, after reading this you may ask, well, for someone who has such a hands-off approach, why on earth would you decide to build your whole career around investments?

The answer is…I didn't. During my time working for an asset manager I realised it was possible to build wealth by contributing smaller amounts over long time periods. It was my introduction to dollar-cost averaging, and the realisation that investing wasn't just for the wealthy; it was something I could do. Naturally, I asked myself why don't more people invest? The answer is that some people don't know this is the way to build wealth.

Many people who could dramatically improve financial outcomes for themselves and for their children and grandchildren have not been exposed to their version of the blueprint. It is satisfying to be able to make this information accessible to everyday Australians and all types of investors.

(continued)

My investment philosophy is individual to me. It's investing my way. It has evolved over time, and I imagine it will continue to evolve. The beauty of investing is being able to take on other perspectives, many of which are those of our readers and listeners on our podcast. It's understanding what works for you and understanding that all of this is really just a journey to create a better life for yourself and your loved ones.

Mark's investment strategy

Given my goals, my investment strategy shouldn't come as a surprise. I document and share my strategy here but it's not the whole story. Picking one investment strategy necessitates rejecting others. This can be difficult because many of the advocates for those strategies are passionate and articulate.

I've followed the same strategy for close to 25 years now and over time the conviction that I'm doing the right thing for me has only increased. But that's not to say there aren't other strategies that can be successful. Part of choosing an investment strategy is having the humility to accept that other people will be successful — sometimes much more successful — doing different things.

On the surface it may appear that Shani and I are taking dramatically different approaches. Yet fundamentally we have a great deal in common. Shani bought sexy-sounding funds when she was younger. I was overly impressed with financial-speak that led me down some wrong paths. What I mean by financial-speak is the language many professional investors use to communicate. Their descriptions of investments are often filled with jargon, confusing terminology and financial metrics many everyday investors may only tenuously grasp. When I was younger I read up on any terms I didn't understand

and as my knowledge grew I felt I was being given the key to an exclusive club. I'm no longer impressed by that exclusivist language. I think the smartest people explain complex terms simply and that this reveals both confidence and humility.

The more income I earn, the more choices I have. Yet, like Shani, I've found a simple strategy often works best.

In my job I spend a lot of time speaking and listening to professional investors. For the most part they are very smart and work very hard, but earning a return that exceeds the index every single year is so difficult that most of them fail. Morningstar's Active Passive Barometer shows that only 28 per cent of active managers beat their passive counterparts over a 10-year period. That is not a good track record.

As part of my investment strategy, I try to assess the long-term prospects of a business to grow earnings and pay dividends. But if I were trying to beat the market every year I would also have to evaluate the short-term prospects for share prices. I would have to identify short-term catalysts that would move share prices. I would have to keep abreast of the economic cycle, predict where it would go and what shares would benefit. And I would have to do all this before other investors could do it.

The game as it is practised by professional investors and mimicked by individual investors is nearly impossible to win. Yet many investors keep playing because they have internalised an unrealistic view of successful investing. In our different ways, Shani and I have come up with straightforward approaches that work. Rather than focusing on beating meaningless benchmarks over the short term we pursue long-term goals. Unlike most investors who trade more frequently, we are buy-and-hold investors. Ultimately, we're trying to be what most people aren't — patient and consistent.

(continued)

I've incorporated my approach into my investment strategy, codifying it to keep me on track. The way I invest is not exciting; in fact, it is deliberately boring. Like Shani, I'm controlling what I can control, and for me that's mostly my behaviour.

I want to build passive income in my non-retirement accounts. To achieve my goal I will purchase income-producing assets that provide a stable and growing income stream. I'll allocate 90 per cent of my portfolio to growth assets and 10 per cent to defensive assets.

My competitive advantage stems from behavioural and structural edge. Taking advantage of this requires a focus on finding great dividend-paying companies with long-term competitive advantages. This means I will purchase investments at attractive valuations and hold them for the long term to take advantage of dividend growth. Structured decision making that enables me to take advantage of my sources of edge is the key to my success.

I will invest in individual shares, ETFs and funds. I'll avoid actively managed ETFs and funds and those that are likely to generate high levels of realised capital gains due to index construction and rebalancing policies.

I will focus on investments in high-quality, non-cyclical companies with moats, strong finances, low business risk and acceptable dividend payout ratios. My goal is for the yield of my overall portfolio to exceed the global market, but more importantly I want growth in dividends, so I will balance income growth in individual holdings with higher current dividend yields. My goal is for each investment I buy to have dividend growth that exceeds inflation in order to increase my purchasing power from passive income over time.

I do not want any single share to represent more than 5 per cent of my portfolio either in market value or percentage of income. For an ETF I will set limits based on how broadly it is diversified. The purpose is to ensure that any mistakes I make won't impact the income my portfolio generates or the value of my portfolio to such an extent that I won't be able to achieve my goals.

I will examine my allocation to growth and defensive assets on an annual basis and will consider making a change if the allocation is 5 per cent above or below my target.

I will try to avoid rebalancing by selling a position and will do so only if I cannot adjust my portfolio by redirecting dividends and new savings.

I will change individual holdings if they have demonstrated conclusively they no longer fit my original thesis and my security-selection criteria. I will wait at least a week before selling anything to make sure I am not making emotional decisions.

Key takeaways

This chapter's central focus has been the exercise that helped you develop your investment strategy. Much of the supporting theory was introduced in previous chapters. The key lesson is that your investment strategy will be your north star on your investment journey. It will provide you with guidance on what to buy (and sell), how these transactions connect to your financial goals and how/when to monitor your portfolio.

You now have a personalised investment strategy, a plan that will enable you to accomplish the goal you have defined. And you now have the structure in place to avoid the mistakes too many investors make.

Finding the right investments for you

Ellen Langer, a professor of psychology at Harvard, is known as the 'mother of mindfulness'. Apparently that's meant as a compliment. In addition to starting the study of mindfulness in an academic setting, and giving birth to the modern mindfulness movement, Langer coined the expression 'the illusion of control' to describe our tendency to overestimate our ability to control events.

Langer performed a series of experiments to test her hypothesis. In one experiment her test subjects convinced themselves they had a better chance of winning a lottery when they picked the tickets themselves. In another, they thought they could trigger a random reward by creating intricate sequences of button pressing.

In our experience, investors like to come up with 'systems' to pick what to buy or sell in their portfolio. These systems encourage irrational decisions because they instil the belief that our system gives us more control over the outcome. The movements of markets are random over the short term; there's no system that can predict what happens. But by focusing on the long term, you can have more control over your investment outcomes.

We've waited a while to start talking about investments. The reason that we've chosen to finish the book with the subject of picking investments should be apparent to readers by now. We don't think they are the most important part of investing. The most important parts are asset allocation and controlling your behaviour. We've sought to ensure you get both right by creating a goal and a strategy and thinking through your personal financial philosophy.

While we explore investments you might choose to go back and refine your strategy. That's perfectly fine. It will take time to craft your investment strategy. For now it's time to find investments that will help you achieve your goals.

Shani says...

Most investors jump immediately to this part. It's hard not to. In the past 15 years you could have invested successfully in almost anything. Markets don't work like this over the long run, though. There will always be a downturn; there will always be investments – or sectors of the market – that fail to meet your expectations. Start with a strong awareness of what you are actually looking for in an investment. Determining 'the best performing investment' just won't cut it and isn't a sustainable way to invest. Pick investments that suit your goals, but also suit your behaviour and your edge. When you have a strong understanding of what you are trying to achieve, and you seek out an investment that fits those criteria, you will be better positioned for success.

Picking investments

This is not a stock and ETF picking book. It is about achieving financial freedom by creating a personalised strategy to achieve your goals. It's about designing your finances around what you want out of life. We've emphasised that the biggest influence on the investment results you achieve is not the investments you pick, however counterintuitive that may sound. Poor behaviour and the wrong asset allocation will outweigh any skills you have in picking stocks, funds and ETFs.

Instead of describing a discounted cash flow approach to value a share like a professional investor, or some gimmick for picking ETFs, we're going to explain the fundamentals of shares, funds and ETFs — not what they are but what you should consider when picking them.

No matter what type of investment you are considering, the most important thing is to make sure the investment fits your strategy and aligns with your goals. In *The Paradox of Choice*, Barry Schwartz observed, 'Learning to choose is hard. Learning to choose well is harder. And learning to choose well in a world of unlimited possibilities is harder still, perhaps too hard.' As an investor you have an abundance of choice. This is often characterised as a good thing. We're not so sure.

Once the basics have been covered, choice becomes problematic for investors. When there are lots of choices providers of investment products must work harder to get chosen. This means more niche products and more products that appeal to our base emotions.

We see sensible ideas like John Bogle's championing of passive investing corrupted by narrower and narrower indexes. Worst of all, investor behaviour is negatively impacted by choice and the aggressive marketing that is needed for an investment to stand out.

This is why it's so beneficial to eliminate large categories of investments. Mark has eliminated actively managed funds and ETFs, bonds and any share that doesn't pay a dividend. Shani has eliminated all individual shares. This shrinks the universe of options, which makes things easier. Making commitments to an investment strategy that eliminates choices is freeing because it allows you to ignore all other sources of temptation. You've taken this step, which should make things easier for you. Now let's get into some of the specific types of investments.

Shares

There are two critical items for any investor who owns shares to keep top of mind — and this includes investors who own a fund or ETF that holds shares. Every book on investing reminds readers that a share represents partial ownership of a business. After this box-checking exercise, many books shift into a bewildering examination of financial ratios or nonsensical charts that seem to contradict this foundational point.

We'll focus on the business part. It's important to remember that all businesses are different and that they are constantly competing against other businesses. This seems obvious in the real world, but many people lose sight of it in the investing world.

Some companies are riskier than others

At a fundamental level some businesses are riskier than others. This is neither a good nor a bad thing. As investors we all take on risk to earn a return. How much risk we take on is a function of what we are trying to accomplish and our plan for doing it.

Once again, this is why you need goals and a strategy. We've already got that out of the way, which makes it easier to figure out what types of companies are for you.

The value of any company is the future cash flows the company generates. Those cash flows have value because the company can do lots of different things with them. They could expand the business by investing in new employees or new equipment or more marketing. New products or services could be created or existing ones improved by investment in research and development. Debt could be paid down, reducing interest expenses. Shareholders could be rewarded with dividends and buybacks. Another company could be purchased.

Simplistically, all that matters for a company is the size of the cash flows it generates and what is done with the cash flows. Success in this endeavour will drive the performance of the share price.

Logic dictates that the inherent risk of any business is the unpredictability of the cash flows that will be generated by the company in the future. If the company generates more cash flows than investors expect, that is a good thing. If the company underperforms expectations, the share price will likely suffer. To understand the risk of a business requires understanding the factors that influence future cash flows. These factors vary from business to business and by industry.

For some businesses, their future cash flows are influenced by a wide range of factors. Some of these factors are in their control; many are outside their control. The economic climate, factors influencing pricing, consumer tastes and the actions of competitors may be influences outside the control of a business.

More debt means a riskier company. Debt is often sold as an enabler of choice. In reality, for both individuals and businesses, it limits future options. A heavily indebted company may lose the flexibility to respond effectively to an unexpected crisis or take advantage of opportunities.

For a company with predictable cash flow generation all that may be needed is a moderate level of management competence to stay on the right path. Warren Buffett famously said, 'I try to buy stock in businesses that are so wonderful that an idiot can run them. Because sooner or later, one will.'

A company with a wide range of factors influencing future performance has more potential outcomes, especially if many of those factors are outside the company's control. Future outcomes are less predictable.

If all goes well, buying shares in a company with a wide range of future outcomes could be enormously profitable. Investors likely wouldn't anticipate such a fortuitous outcome, and their expectations would be exceeded. Conversely, if even a couple things go wrong that same company could go out of business. In this case an investor could lose their entire investment.

Large, mature companies generally have more predictable future outcomes than small companies. Typically they operate in a range of different countries and sell lots of different product and service lines. This means they have less exposure to an issue with any single product or the economic conditions in any single country. Much of a mature company's products are likely established and proven, which is how the company got big in the first place. The opposite is true for small emerging companies. They may operate in a single country or region and may have a single, unproven product. Neither profile is good or bad. The point is they are different, and the expectations of investors are baked into the share price.

The types of products sold by the company can increase or decrease the predictability of future outcomes. Companies that sell products that consumers need regardless of the economic conditions are referred to as non-cyclical or defensive. In all economic conditions people need basic household goods, food, healthcare and electricity. These companies can thrive in any economic environment, which eliminates another factor that influences their results.

The fortunes of cyclical companies change in different economic environments. For instance, a company selling luxury goods would do well when people are feeling optimistic about their financial prospects. They don't do as well when the economy is doing poorly. This makes their future outcomes less predictable, as the economy is another factor to worry about.

Table 10.1 (overleaf) groups different industrial sectors into defensive (not influenced by the business cycle), sensitive (somewhat influenced by the business cycle) and cyclical (heavily influenced by the business cycle) categories. Each sector contains companies that have similar business models. Sector information for each share is available at a variety of financial sites on the internet, including Morningstar.

Think about your investment goals, strategy and temperament and about the level of business risk that's right for you. The more predictable future cash flows are, the fewer surprises may be in store for you as an investor. Companies with unpredictable future cash flows could do very well or so poorly they go out of business. Over the long run share prices follow the performance of the business.

Table 10.1: stock sectors by economic influence

Economic influence	Stock sector
Cyclical	Basic materials
	Consumer cyclical
	Financial services
	Real estate
Sensitive	Communication services
	Energy
	Industrials
	Technology
Defensive	Consumer defensive
	Healthcare
	Utilities

In his investment strategy Mark favours low business risk and non-cyclical companies with predictable futures. That's because his goal is to generate safe and growing income. A business whose results swing wildly is unlikely to produce safe and growing dividends. That's one example of how a goal and investment strategy lines up with the types of investments considered.

Case Study: The rise of Google

Outcomes often appear inevitable in retrospect, when in reality they are anything but. In 1996, two PHD students at Stanford University named Larry Page and Sergey Brin started a research project on creating a better internet search engine. At the time, the search market was fragmented, with AltaVista controlling around a quarter of internet searches. Excite followed with a 15 per cent market share, Lycos at 12 per cent and Yahoo at 8 per cent.

Google was founded in 1998 based on the results of this research project. By then the search market was starting to concentrate, with AltaVista, Lycos and Yahoo handling 50 per cent of total internet searches.

At the turn of the millennium, Google was starting to make its mark, with just over a 10 per cent share of total searches. Yahoo was now the clear leader with a 20 per cent share, but MSN, the new entrant by software giant Microsoft, had been gaining ground and held a 12.5 per cent share. By 2003, Google had taken over the number-one ranking, pulling just ahead of Yahoo, MSN and AOL.

In 2007, Google hit 50 per cent market share, and from there it consolidated its position as the number-one search engine. Today it makes up roughly 83 per cent of internet search volume, despite not operating in China.

This incredible journey was far from preordained. Thousands of factors contributed to Google's rise, including its smart decisions, poor decisions by better-funded rivals and shifts in the way consumers purchased and researched products and how companies marketed them.

Shifts in the way governments approached anti-trust provisions, with little initial concern about Google's growing market power, abetted this rise. The availability and scale of funding from private and public investors also facilitated Google's growth. The decision by Larry Page and Sergey Brin to put their egos aside and hire an experienced CEO in 2001 assuaged the investor community and set them on the pathway to going public in 2004.

Throughout this early period, the range of possible outcomes for Google was immense. To progress from a research study to one of the largest companies in the world took a lot of skill and a lot of luck. It took the efforts of countless individuals,

(continued)

governments and companies to create the internet as we know it today. It also took a shift in the behaviour of billions of people around the world.

Was creating a better search engine a key factor in this growth? Of course. But history is littered with better products that didn't make it. Products that didn't come around at the right time. Products that didn't have the external factors that facilitated their growth into a dominant position. Better products that were sabotaged by poor decision making and bad luck.

A $1000 investment in Google when it went public roughly 20 years ago would result in a position worth $58 180 today. It could easily have been worth nothing if just a few things had been different. This was a lottery ticket, not a preordained and predictable outcome.

Investing is a probabilistic enterprise. The more factors that need to go right for a company and the lower probability of each of those factors going right contribute to the chances of a particular outcome occurring.

For instance, say ten factors contributed to Google's rise. If there was a 25 per cent chance that each of those ten factors went right, the chances of that happening were less than one in a million. To be exact, a 0.00009536743 per cent chance.

If only some of those factors went Google's way, perhaps it would have been a somewhat successful company battling it out with Bing and Yahoo for advertising dollars. 'Google' would not have entered the lexicon.

Competition

If you've read anything about investing, you've probably heard the term *moat*. Despite the popularity of moats many people find the term's meaning nebulous. Moats can be thought of as a mythical creature of investing. We are told they exist. We see signs of them everywhere, but — try as we might — identifying a moat seems to remain just out of reach.

The term is generally attributed to Warren Buffett, which no doubt contributes to its popularity. If the most famous investor in the world cares about something, then perhaps we should too. A moat is a sustainable competitive advantage. The image of a moat as a watery barrier protecting a castle is apt. A moat protects a company from ruinous competition. To offer effective protection the moat must be sustainable. This is the tricky part of identifying a moat. Some companies benefit from a first mover advantage but without the protection of a moat those advantages will be eroded over time by competitors eager to seize an attractive opportunity.

Evaluating a share means evaluating a business. And any evaluation of a business starts with the environment in which the company operates. For most publicly traded companies that environment is capitalism. And capitalism is synonymous with competition. When capitalism functions properly competition benefits consumers. Companies invest in creating better products and services for us to buy, and they compete on price so we get better deals.

The problem is that competition isn't great for companies. To compete with another company often means spending more money on research and development and on marketing. It means reduced profit margins as prices on goods and services are cut. The combination of that spending and lower prices means lower profits. That's not what we want to see as investors.

The impact of competition shows up in the financial statements. A company funds itself using loans from banks by issuing debt and by selling shares. This funding has a cost and when it is invested in growing the business it earns a return. If that return is below the cost, eventually the company will go bankrupt. If the return is higher than the cost of capital, the company thrives over the long term.

These outlier scenarios are fairly rare. Eventually most companies' returns roughly match their cost of capital. This is the impact of competition's eroding returns. Remember that a company is a self-perpetuating entity that will constantly keep struggling to grow.

Earning returns that match the cost of capital is not a great outcome for investors. However, the company can keep growing and keep paying management and employees as long as it doesn't let the return on invested capital dip below the cost of capital. This is a maintainable if not ideal situation.

A great business earns higher internal returns than its competitors in the same industry. It keeps more of its revenue through higher margins. That's the pathway for compounding returns over decades.

There's no magic formula for identifying a moat. We can look back at companies that earned higher margins and higher returns on invested capital. But that's the past. What matters is what happens in the future.

Finding a moat involves doing something that has become increasingly rare. It involves thinking. Put down your computer or your phone and think about a business. Start with a product or service that you, your family or friends use regularly. Think about what influences your purchasing decisions. Think about what would cause you to buy a competing product or service.

Would you switch to a competing product or service if it offers a slightly lower price? If the answer is yes, there likely isn't a moat.

Is this a product or service where innovations are constantly causing you to switch to a better offering? Once again, if the answer is yes, there likely isn't a moat.

Does the product or service become more valuable to you because more people use it? If not, there likely isn't a moat.

Think about what it takes to deliver that product and service. What influences the cost of providing that good or service? Are there efficiencies available to companies operating on a larger scale?

What prevents or inhibits new competitors entering the industry and providing a new competing good or service that you might consider buying?

Answering those questions will offer clues to the competitive environment facing a company. Morningstar has identified five sources of competitive advantage. Companies that exhibit one or more of these sources have a moat. This framework can guide your thinking.

NETWORK EFFECT

A network effect occurs when the value of a company's goods or services increases for both new and existing users as more people use them. A network effect is often found in technology-enabled services such as social media, payment platforms, communications platforms and e-commerce.

In all these cases the whole point of the services is to interact or connect with other individuals or companies. The more connections available, the more value a user derives from the service.

INTANGIBLE ASSETS

Investors often focus on tangible assets that are reflected on the balance sheet. However, just because something can't be seen and quantified doesn't mean it isn't valuable. Patents, brands, regulatory licences and other intangible assets can prevent competitors from duplicating a company's products or allow the company to charge higher prices.

This moat source is broad and encompasses many different competitive environments. Intangible assets can be bestowed by government bodies to encourage innovation in the case of patents, which includes drugs sold by pharmaceutical companies or new technology.

Many products and services can benefit from strong brands that induce consumers to spend more on otherwise equivalent offerings and maintain market share over multiple decades.

Finally, there are cases where local and national governments grant limited or exclusive licences to certain businesses. They may do this in exchange for a significant investment in the case of publicly useful infrastructure or to restrict availability in the case of a casino.

COST ADVANTAGE

Firms with a structural cost advantage can either undercut competitors on price while earning similar margins, or they can charge market-level prices while earning relatively high margins. In general, cost advantages stem from scale, from firms that can spread their fixed costs over a huge customer base.

SWITCHING COSTS

Pricing power is maintained when it would be too expensive or inconvenient to stop using a company's products or services. For some goods and services, it is easy to switch to a competing product. For commonly purchased items competing products may be simply a shelf away.

However, some goods and services require significant effort, such as switching a bank account or changing software that is embedded within a personal or business process. Once a company has captured significant market share it is difficult to pry customers away, as the effort involved in switching providers requires the inducement of overwhelmingly better features or prices.

EFFICIENT SCALE

If a niche market is effectively served by one or a handful of companies, *efficient scale* may apply, when competitors decide it isn't worth entering the market given the small number of customers.

For example, a pharmaceutical company has developed an effective treatment for a relatively small number of patients afflicted with a condition, or an expensive piece of infrastructure such as a railroad supports a targeted market.

Mark's investment strategy includes looking to buy companies with moats. This criterion aligns with his goal of generating a safe and growing income stream. Investing for dividends means holding for the long term, and a company with a moat is more likely to retain a strong position against competitors over the long term.

Case Study: Moats matter

A few real-life examples bring the concept of a moat to life. The Australian banking industry is notoriously concentrated, with the big four banks capturing sizable portions of the market.

The industry benefits from scale as the fixed costs of branches and technology systems can be spread more efficiently

(continued)

across large customer bases. Their size also allows them to access funding at advantageous rates.

Banking products also have high switching costs. Customers typically utilise multiple services by banks including various accounts and credit products. Direct deposit and bill pay services entwine banking within day-to-day life.

Each of the big four banks has received a wide moat rating from our analysts stemming from cost advantages and switching costs. We can see the impact when we compare the financial statements of the large, dominant banks and mid-sized banks.

For instance, Judo Bank is a relative newcomer that has focused on small and medium-sized business lending. The company has grown but is at a decided disadvantage in the competitive landscape of the banking industry.

Judo suffers from a smaller loan book and higher funding and operational costs in relation to larger competitors. One measure often used to evaluate banks is return on equity. This shows how much of the bank's shareholder's equity (equal to assets minus its borrowings and other liabilities) is being turned into fresh profits. The preference here is for a higher number, and for a consistently high number at that. Judo has a return on equity of around 5 per cent. The major banks have low double-digit returns on equity.

Judo recently issued debt at a cost of 6.5 per cent over the one-month bank bill swap rate. National Australia Bank issued similar debt a few months ago at 2.2 per cent over the same rate. The combination of these factors means that Judo experiences a cost-to-income ratio of 54 per cent. The major banks are in the mid-forties despite a more extensive product range. The differences in these ratios will accrue to investors over the long term.

Where returns come from

Following the commentary on the sharemarket can be confusing. We are inundated with data, financial metrics and esoteric approaches to finding shares to buy. One way to cut through this noise is to consider the only three sources of returns. We are always surprised that investors are not more thoughtful about the drivers of returns. It really does help to clarify your thinking on an investment you are considering. We've used Apple as an example to illustrate the three drivers of returns so you can evaluate shares you hold.

The first source is dividends. It should be obvious this is a source of returns, as a dividend is cash in your pocket. Dividends make up a meaningful part of total returns, especially in dividend-obsessed Australia. Dividends are a by-product of earnings. You need to earn money to return it to shareholders. And you need to grow earnings to grow dividends.

In Apple's case the dividend yield has been quite low. On Morningstar.com.au we looked up the yield of Apple shares for each of the past five years (table 10.2). Dividends clearly didn't play much of a role in the returns.

The second driver is changes in valuation. As a partial owner of a company, a shareholder is interested in how much that company earns. If what we want as investors is earnings, we can view the price we pay for a share in relation to earnings. That's why there is so much commentary about the price to earnings or P/E ratio. At any given time it represents what an investor is willing to pay for earnings.

Table 10.2: Apple's (AAPL) dividend 2020–24

Apple Inc.	2020	2021	2022	2023	2024
Dividend yield	0.61%	0.49%	0.70%	0.49%	0.40%

Source: Morningstar data

How much investors are willing to pay for earnings can change over time. If investors expect earnings to grow faster in the future, it is rational to pay higher valuation levels. The opposite is true as well. If investors are negative about the prospects for growth, they will pay lower valuation levels.

Sometimes investors get a little too enthusiastic about the prospects of a company. They can get overexcited and fall victim to greed. This is when bubbles form and individual shares and the market trade at higher valuations. Sometimes investors get irrationally fearful and valuation levels of certain shares and the market fall.

The most important thing to remember about valuations is that they are based on expectations. Changes in valuations are all about what investors think will happen in the future. Share price changes based on valuation changes are a result not of how a company performs but of how the company performs *in comparison to expectations*. More on this later.

Table 10.3 shows Apple's price to earnings ratio over the past five years. In this case you can see that it dipped in 2021 and 2022 before rebounding. That was a time when the market was not doing well and clearly Apple investors were pulling back on the valuation level they were willing to pay.

The third driver is earnings growth (table 10.4). If we are willing to pay 20 times earnings for a share earning $1 and are still willing to pay 20 times earnings when the company makes $2, the share price will double.

Table 10.3: Apple's (AAPL) price-to-earnings ratio 2020–24

	2020	2021	2022	2023	2024
Price to earnings ratio	40.45	31.65	21.27	31.41	41.19

Source: Morningstar data

Table 10.4: Apple's (AAPL) diluted net income 2020–24

	2020	2021	2022	2023	2024
Diluted net income	$57411	$94680	$99803	$96995	$93736

Source: Morningstar data

Looking at earnings provides more context to the changes in valuation levels. Earnings were down significantly in 2020, which makes sense given the pandemic. That higher price to earnings rate in 2020 was investors ignoring the disruption to the economy. Then when earnings rebounded the valuation levels fell. Overall, not a great five years of earnings growth other than the bounce-back year of 2021.

Remember, dividends, changes in valuation and earnings growth are the three sources of returns. There are myriad reasons that factor into dividend levels, the valuation investors are willing to pay and earnings, but we shouldn't lose sight of the foundational drivers of returns (table 10.5).

If we look at the returns per year over the past five years, we can see that Apple has been on a strong run with the exception of the 2022 bear market. The main driver at the tail end of the five-year period was the increase in valuation even as earnings stagnated and dividends contributed little to the total return. This provides perspective on how to evaluate Apple's prospects going forward. Can valuations increase from already high levels? Can earnings growth start up again? This gives you some context on which to base additional research.

Table 10.5: Apple's (AAPL) annual performance 2020–24

	2020	2021	2022	2023	2024
Annual performance	80.75%	33.82%	–26.83%	48.18%	30.07%

Source: Morningstar data

The three factors that drive returns don't offer some magic formula that identifies which shares to buy and which to avoid. However, they do inject some common sense into the process of trying to evaluate a business. We all want to buy shares with high returns. When considering buying any share it is worth mapping out where the return will come from. If a share has performed well in the past, it's useful to know where those returns came from.

The hardest thing for many investors to grasp is changes in valuation levels and the role expectations play in that process. We invest based on our anticipation of the future. Expectations of the future are baked into security prices. If investors have high expectations for the prospects of a company, the shares will trade at a higher valuation. That isn't necessarily a bad thing — as long as those expectations are met — but it should be obvious that the higher the expectations, the harder they will be to meet and exceed.

For example, when the economy is strong and growing it is good for company earnings. But shares often rally significantly prior to an economic turn. This can create cognitive dissonance for investors. The economic environment experienced from day to day is very different from the performance of the stock market, which is already looking down the road towards an economic recovery. This can be hard for many people to wrap their head around.

Mark often uses the global financial crisis as an example when speaking to investors. The US stock market rally began six months before unemployment peaked in the US. It's important to remember that it would have required clairvoyance at the time to know this actually represented the peak. Investors who waited for clear signs of an improving economy missed out on significant gains that grew into one of the greatest bull markets in history.

In retrospect it seemed obvious that it was a good time to invest. Market commentators will look back and note that shares were cheap and point to the rally that followed as justification for their view that it was an obvious time to invest. We take comfort in the logic of this argument and assume we would have acted rationally and purchased shares at the bottom of the market.

At the time, however, shares were not cheap because earnings had fallen in response to the economic crisis. What made them cheap in retrospect was the economic revival and the resulting earnings recovery. There are countless examples of instances when the market has rallied on hopes of a recovery that never happened. This is called a bear market rally.

How to use this information to pick shares

We've outlined the main things we think you should consider when picking a share. The type of business you invest in and the competitive environment it operates within will determine the results for the business over the long term. How the business performs will influence the share price by impacting the amount paid out in dividends, the growth of earnings and the expectations of investors. All the influences we've discussed — from the spectrum of different risks that businesses face to the impact of competition to the three drivers of returns — have one thing in common. They are all things that will influence a share price over the long term, though they will have little influence on short-term returns. The following observation, which Warren Buffet attributed to Benjamin Graham, is one of the most quoted aphorisms in the investing world: 'In the short run, the market is a voting machine but in the long run it is a weighing machine.' It's good advice. We have better things to do than focus on how investors are going to vote on any particular day of the year. Focusing on the long term is much more useful.

Case Study: On the small number of successful investments

In a 2018 study, Hendrik Bessembinder of Arizona State University reviewed every share in the US since 1926 and found that 90 shares have accounted for half the total return of the stock market. All of the wealth was created by the thousand top-performing shares; 96 per cent of shares in the US earned a return that matched a one-month Treasury bill.

According to financial commentator Ashley Owen, 37000 companies have listed on Australian stock exchanges since the late 1800s; 33500 of them have delisted, which rendered them worthless; and 65 per cent of the companies ever listed in Australia have suffered 100 per cent losses. If one of those companies made up a significant portion of your portfolio, that 100 per cent loss would likely have been catastrophic.

Every investor will draw their own conclusion from this data. To us it seems obvious that the secret to getting the highest performance is to buy individual shares. However, to do this an investor needs to find those elusive '10-baggers'. This isn't impossible but it is really hard. If you take this route, you should have a strategy to build a portfolio that can outperform. If you can't at least articulate your competitive advantage over other investors, it might be better to stick with ETFs.

The other lesson is that a lot of investments are purely speculative. The companies that didn't make it are the ones that disappeared. Yes, some investors picked the right speculative company and did well, but most investors lost a lot of money. Both of us avoid speculative investments. Even owning a diversified portfolio of speculative investments is likely to end badly. Slow and steady wins the race.

How to evaluate funds and ETFs

Different approaches are needed when choosing between a passive ETF or fund that tracks an index and an active ETF or fund that relies on manager skill to pick securities.

Passive ETFs and funds

An ETF or fund is a product. A company has created that product to try to make money. The more people who invest in an ETF or fund, the more money the company will make. Always keep this in mind. Some people are incentivised to come up with compelling-sounding ETFs and funds to encourage you to invest in their products.

Passive ETFs track an index, but there are big differences between different types of ETFs and funds. There are broad ETFs and funds that track well-known indexes such as the ASX 200 and the S&P 500. There are also factor and thematic ETFs tracking specialised indexes that are designed to capture a certain characteristic or theme that investors may want exposure to.

Each of those indexes has rules that dictate what securities are selected, the weightings of those securities and when changes are made. If you don't understand how an index works, you don't understand what you are investing in. This guarantees you will not achieve your goals except by dumb luck. If you don't understand how an investment works, don't buy it.

Beware of labels. ETFs with similar names may take very different approaches. Some ETF names are meant to capture investor attention but are unable to match the label effectively.

The good news is that indexes come in all shapes and sizes. Some are simple. Almost any investor can understand them. The ASX

200 includes the 200 largest companies in Australia and weights them based on their size. Changes are made only if the 201st biggest company becomes larger than the 200th. That's an index that requires little investing knowledge to understand.

Some indexes are very complex. Securities with certain characteristics are included, such as value shares or quality shares, or a certain theme is captured like robotics or AI. If you don't understand how these indexes work, just don't invest in those ETFs. Selecting broad index ETFs is a proven way to build wealth and achieve your financial goals.

Active ETFs and funds

Active ETFs are managed by an individual or a team of professional investors. There are certain guidelines that dictate what securities they can pick. But ultimately you are relying on the skill of professional managers. This is harder to assess for the average investor, but it is important to understand the strategy. Tread carefully with actively managed ETFs and know that most managers underperform the index.

Cash

Figuring out what to do with cash is one of the easiest financial decisions you make. You compare interest rates at the bank, and you choose the highest one with the product that best suits your circumstances. For example, many high-interest savings accounts have stipulations about mandatory investment amounts and frequency. Choose one that works.

Because cash is relatively easy in this way, it is more useful to speak about when and how it may fit into your portfolio. Let's start with risk. We've discussed how the investment industry views risk and how investors should view risk.

Remember, the investment industry measures risk as volatility, or how much the price of a security or portfolio bounces around. One asset has no volatility: cash. And that means cash carries no risk — if we accept that risk and volatility are synonymous. This means if you have $1 in the bank, it's going to stay as $1 — and some change with interest. The Financial Claims Scheme (FCS) is an Australian Government program that protects cash balances up to $250 000 in banks, which means that in the unlikely scenario that one of the banks goes out of business, you don't lose the money in your bank account up to that amount.

As investors, we understand that there is a relationship between risk and reward. If we take on more risk, we should have higher expectations of reward. For instance, shares have higher volatility and correspondingly higher expected returns. Cash has no volatility and the lowest expected return of any asset class.

It's important to understand the role cash plays in your investment goals to know whether it should be included in your portfolio and to what degree.

The major issue with cash as an asset class is inflation. Inflation reduces the purchasing power of money, and over the long term, interest does not offer you much more than inflation. If we go back 200 years, the real or inflation-adjusted return on cash is 1.73 per cent. A common theme that we have tried to stress in this book is that investing is a necessity if you want to create a comfortable life for yourself. This is particularly the case in retirement when you will be supporting yourself on your savings.

Let's look at an example. You are 28 years old and planning on retiring at 65. You want to support yourself in retirement for another 25 years until you're 90. You want 70 per cent of your salary in annual retirement spending. If you just keep your savings in cash you need to save over 47 per cent of your salary for the next 37 years to achieve this goal.

This example is consistent with one of our themes. Cash won't get you there. Since you are reading this investing book, we hope you don't need much more convincing of that.

We are of course looking at cash in the context of an investment portfolio that is designed to help you achieve a longer-term goal. We're not talking about an emergency fund. An emergency fund should be in cash, as its purpose is to protect your portfolio by enabling you to deal with unexpected events without having to sell off long-term assets. You should try to avoid any situations in which you are forced to sell anything except at a time of your choosing. An emergency fund is non-negotiable regardless of how low interest rates may be.

None of this means you should not hold cash. There are many reasons for investors to hold cash. Your portfolio can be in an accumulation phase or a de-accumulation phase. Accumulation is when you are saving and investing. De-accumulation is when you are using your portfolio to pay for your goal. That can happen in an instant if your goal is a deposit on a home, or over decades in retirement.

In the accumulation phase, cash will lower your volatility while reducing the expected return of your portfolio. The more cash you hold, the less your portfolio will bounce around. It will also lower the long-term return you can expect to receive. In any given year the market can fall significantly. In those cases cash would improve your return, but over the long term this would not be the case.

Some investors choose to make tactical allocations to cash. Strategic asset allocation is your long-term asset allocation target and the output from the process of defining your goal and calculating your required rate of return. You may decide you need 90 per cent growth assets and 10 per cent cash to achieve your goal. A tactical asset allocation may be a short-term deviation from this strategic asset allocation that you make based on market conditions. Making a tactical asset allocation decision should not be done lightly, because regardless of the rationale this is market timing.

In many cases a tactical allocation decision involves cash. An average investor is probably not going to move 2 per cent of their portfolio from listed property to infrastructure because they see some anomaly in the relative positioning of those two asset classes. It's more likely someone will invest extra cash in shares if they see an opportunity or build up a bit of cash if they don't see opportunities. Much of the poor investor behaviour that is so damaging to long-term returns results from tactical asset allocation decisions.

Another use for cash is ensuring you de-risk your portfolio as you approach your investment goal. This is because staying fully invested is very risky. Looking at the S&P 500 index of the largest US companies from 1986 to 2021, there have been negative returns over one-year rolling periods 18 per cent of the time. During the same stretch there have been rolling three-year losses 12 per cent of the time. You don't want your portfolio to drop and risk being unable to achieve your goal.

The rule of thumb from the industry is to go to cash two years before you need to achieve your lump-sum goal. We're not too sure about this. The real question for investors here is: what are the consequences if you don't hit your goals? This can dictate how conservative you need to be. For example, if Mark is saving up for a black-market liver to save his life, he should probably go to cash.

For a home purchase, you may be able to delay the purchase if the market drops.

For de-accumulation, the risk is retiring in a bear market. If the market drops as you retire, it can have a profound impact on how long you can go without running out of money. From the moment you retire you start to withdraw money from your portfolio. If the market is also dropping, you are selling low to fund those withdrawals. You have less assets invested to help you recover. In this case, the real risk is selling your retirement portfolio when you don't want to — the same thing you're trying to avoid with an emergency fund.

One way to address this risk is by holding cash in your portfolio. The cash will do two things. It will dampen volatility, which means your portfolio won't fluctuate as much. Cash can also fund your withdrawals so you don't have to sell other assets in a down market.

Cash can be used to de-risk, as a tactical allocation tool and to fund withdrawals. Although investors should be wary about the low returns from the asset class, it can be a useful tool in your investment portfolio in a multitude of ways.

Why Shani doesn't hold cash

There are a few reasons why I don't hold cash. But I should begin by saying that I do maintain an emergency fund. So when I speak about not holding cash, I'm speaking purely about my investment portfolio. I categorise my emergency fund as insurance rather than as an investment. It is not included when I calculate my portfolio performance or assigned to achieving any particular financial goal. In short, my aversion to holding cash is not a recommendation to chuck your emergency fund into the sharemarket. An emergency fund is critical to the foundations of a strong investment portfolio.

Volatility is also not a concern for me. Cash has a few purposes. It provides liquidity, reduces volatility and can be used for tactical allocations when opportunities arise. None of these uses for cash align with my investment strategy or fit with my goals as they currently stand. I do not need cash to fund any withdrawals from my portfolio. I'm agnostic about market volatility as I don't plan on selling any of my investments for decades. Although I am buying and will do so during times of volatility, I know that markets trend upwards over the long term, and timing the market can significantly reduce returns.

This brings me to tactical allocations. Many fund managers and investors choose to hold on to cash for tactical allocation. Some fund managers feel they must do this to earn their management fee. There's nothing wrong with this if you can get it right, although most managers struggle to do so. Personally, I don't have faith that I can time the market right consistently. The other consideration for professional investors is that they have to consider liquidity in their portfolios. There are hundreds, sometimes thousands, of investors in their funds who have competing goals, financial situations and reactions to market volatility. They have to ensure they have cash so they are able to fund withdrawals in their portfolio. As I'm not a professional manager, I don't need to manage anyone's financial situation, goals or temperament but my own.

My focus is on strategic asset allocation, ensuring that the asset classes and investments I have in my portfolio are aligned with my goals. Rain, hail or shine, I will make my additional investments at set intervals into these set allocations.

Tactical allocations are made based on market conditions. They focus on finding the best opportunities possible. Having a cash allocation helps investors to take advantage of these opportunities.

(continued)

Tactical allocation can be very risky. As previously stated, over the past 30 years, if you missed the S&P 500's 10 best days, your return was cut in half. If you missed the best 30 days over 30 years, your return would be 83 per cent lower. Tactical allocation, especially to cash as a way to keep your powder dry for when opportunities arise, is timing the market.

I would rather invest over the long term and take the guesswork out of picking the best days in the market. I don't think this can be done consistently and I don't think it's worth missing out on the potential returns.

Inflation is also a big concern for me. The fact that I invest on a long time horizon means inflation is likely to erode my capital if it sits in cash.

Diversification is often touted as the only free lunch in investing. A diversified portfolio will always contain a mix of many asset classes, including cash, international and domestic fixed income, alternatives, and international and domestic equities. They will be adjusted proportionally according to risk capacity or risk tolerance.

In reality, outside of academic models, such a complicated mix is often not necessary when constructing a portfolio. Diversification is the process of removing single-security risk from a portfolio. Once that is accomplished many investors pick and choose which asset classes and investments are going to help them reach the outcomes they want, and for me at present that does not include cash. The low returns that cash offers on a long time horizon means I will barely maintain my purchasing power. But I don't want simply to maintain the purchasing power of my money — I want to grow it.

I think it worth noting that my aversion to cash is based on my personal circumstances. It is not a general rejection. Cash is crucial for many investors and can serve several purposes in a portfolio. I don't hold cash now, but that doesn't mean I will never hold it. For example, I'll hold ample cash to fund withdrawals in retirement and provide a buffer against market volatility.

As I get closer to achieving financial goals that have a predetermined end date, my asset class mix will change drastically as I transition from my equity focus to include cash and fixed-income products. As with any part of your investment strategy, think carefully about why you are doing what you are doing and how it helps you accomplish your goals.

Bonds

The bond market is larger than the sharemarket. At the end of 2023, the global sharemarket was worth over US$111 trillion. The global bond market is worth US$119 trillion. Bond markets are not just huge but also complex and diverse.

There are government bonds, corporate bonds, inflation protection bonds, zero coupon bonds … lots to choose from. There's even a Bowie bond, issued by David Bowie when he decided to securitise the future cash flow from his music. A bond is simply a loan, but many bonds are collateralised, meaning they are backed by something. For example, if you get a mortgage, your house is your collateral. Prudential, a large insurance company in the US, bought all the Bowie bonds — $55 million worth. Their collateral was the rights to his music if he didn't pay the bond back.

What's interesting about the Bowie bond is that it was extremely volatile because it coincided with the release of illegal file-sharing applications like Napster and Limewire. This caused Bowie bonds to be downgraded by Moody's, the credit ratings agency, because they were worried that he would no longer make any money from his music. Eventually the bonds matured, and he paid them back in full.

Some bonds can be just as sexy as stocks. Generally, though, bonds have been seen as the boring, conservative part of investors' portfolio. They are considered lower risk and offer lower returns than shares. The name of the game with bonds is risk, as bonds can be so different.

We can start with the risk-free rate. Bonds have credit risk, which is the risk that the bond issuer doesn't pay you back. If you're guaranteed that someone will pay you back, a bond is described as risk free. The risk-free rate generally corresponds with the US Government rate on bonds. It's very difficult for a government to default on their loans because they can literally print the money to pay you back.

There are obviously consequences to this, such as high inflation and the fall in purchasing power of the currency, but technically the debts can be paid and they won't default.

Governments that do default are issuing their bonds in foreign currencies so they can't just print more money. The reason that countries have to issue bonds in foreign currencies is that no-one will allow them to issue them in their own currency for fear of unchecked inflation.

Anything on top of the risk-free rate is generally referred to as a credit spread. Different issuers pay different amounts on their loans because the chances of these issuers paying back their loans vary.

As an investor, the greater the risk that they won't pay you back, the more you're going to demand in interest to make up for that risk. A credit spread describes what investors are willing to accept as additional interest based on the chances that the loans won't be paid back.

Credit agencies such as Moody's and S&P determine how risky these loans are. Moody's AAA rating denotes the highest credit-worthiness rating it offers. Australian Treasury bonds currently have a AAA rating.

The bonds you choose will depend on the amount of risk you want to add to your portfolio and the yield they are offering. Realistically, though, individual bonds are hard to buy for individual investors. Most investors access them through managed funds or ETFs.

Bonds are one place where active managers can go out and earn a return above the index. In Morningstar's 'Active Passive Barometer' report, it is one asset class where active managers have, on average, outperformed their passive peers over the long term. One reason for this is that indexes don't cover the full spectrum of what's out there in the bond market because it is so broad. Therefore active managers have an opportunity to hold positions that make them look very different from the index. They also tend to do a little better in markets that aren't as liquid or as efficient as many equity markets.

Why Mark doesn't hold bonds

We are told that adding bonds to a portfolio lowers risk. The rule of thumb used to be that investors should strive for a 60/40 portfolio. Allocating 40 per cent of your portfolio to bonds is not an insignificant decision.

(continued)

Many people consider a 60/40 portfolio an anachronism. Yet millions of Australians are still allocating a significant amount of their portfolio to bonds. At the end of December 2023, AustralianSuper's balanced option allocated 19 per cent of the portfolio to bonds; 35.9 per cent of the balanced portfolio is in defensive assets. What those defensive assets are is hidden within the maze of undisclosed private investments. Even the high-growth option allocates 11.6 per cent to bonds and 24.5 per cent to defensive assets.

The conventional wisdom that adding bonds to a portfolio lowers risk is true if risk is measured as volatility. In that case a portfolio bouncing around more in price is riskier than one that bounces around less.

When I think about risk to my own portfolio it's not volatility I'm worried about. My portfolio doesn't exist in a theoretical world. It is made up of assets that I want to sell in the future to pay for things I want and need. That means my risk is not having enough money in the future to pay for what I want and need.

Just when I'll need the money to buy things will depend on my personal circumstances. I might want to buy lunch tomorrow. I might need to pay for living expenses in 20 years when I retire. What matters to me is how much the assets I hold are worth when I want to sell them. If I want to sell some assets in 20 years it doesn't matter what they are worth tomorrow and it doesn't matter what they are worth in five years.

Over the long term the real risk I face is that my portfolio won't grow enough to meet my goal. In order to reach my goal I need to save a certain amount, so I need a certain return. I have an estimate of what I need to save and the return I need because I've gone through the goal definition process. The growth of my portfolio needs to be at a certain level in excess of inflation for me to reach my goal. My paper wealth doesn't matter. What matters is how much stuff I can buy with it in the future.

Volatility may be a risk for investors at specific times in their lives. That's because volatility is a short-term risk, and bonds can help solve that problem by reducing volatility. Yet solving the short-term problem introduces a long-term risk to portfolios that many investors are taking on by not interrogating conventional wisdom. That's the risk that you won't earn a return high enough to meet your goals.

According to Vanguard, over the past 30 years Australian bonds have delivered 5.60 per cent annual returns. Australian shares provided 9.10 per cent annual returns and US shares 11.10 per cent. That's a big difference. If you invest $1000 a month for 30 years and earn a 9.10 per cent return annually you'll end up with $1.734 million. A 5.60 per cent return results in $906000.

Obviously, investors are not choosing between a portfolio that's 100 per cent invested in shares or one that's 100 per cent invested in bonds. But this illustrates the trade-off investors are making as the percentage of bonds in a portfolio increases. Over the short term, bonds lower volatility, which for most investors is not a real risk to achieving their long-term goals. Over the long term, they are putting their goals in peril with more bonds.

The real risk embedded in bonds

The returns that were referenced earlier are nominal returns, which means they don't take inflation into account. Those are the returns often quoted by the media and most professional investors. But they are not the returns that matter to investors. As investors we need to care about real, inflation-adjusted returns.

(continued)

If the whole point of investing is to grow our money to buy goods and services in the future, it matters how many of those goods and services we can buy with each dollar. Over the same 30-year period the annual real return from Australian bonds was 2.90 per cent. Australian shares delivered 6.4 per cent annual real returns and US shares 8.4 per cent.

The past 30 years has been a low inflationary environment. The difference between the nominal and real returns was the annual inflation rate of 2.7 per cent. High inflation is a risk that all of us face as investors, as we are focused on real or inflation-adjusted returns. If returns stay the same and inflation increases, our real returns will be lower. Yet inflation isn't a risk that impacts all types of investments equally. It is far more impactful to bonds. This increases their risk far beyond anything measured by volatility.

Anytime you buy an investment there are future expectations baked into the price. For shares the price refers to the valuation. The valuation reflects the expectations about how the company will do in the future. Bonds also have future expectations baked into the price. In this case the expectations are reflected in the yield to maturity of the bond.

The yield of the bond is based on several expectations about the future. The first is the chances of the bond issuer defaulting. But for the sake of this argument we can assume there is a minimal chance of default and that you are buying a high-quality fixed-rate government bond. If I buy a 10-year fixed-rate Australian Government bond at a 5 per cent yield that I plan to hold until maturity, the bet I am really making is on future inflation.

If annual inflation over the next 10 years is more than 5 per cent, my purchase of this bond is a huge mistake. That means by purchasing this bond I am able to buy less stuff in the future. Higher inflation isn't great for shares, yet historically during inflationary environments they have outperformed bonds on both a nominal and a real return basis. And they have done so at a meaningful level.

It makes sense that shares do decently in high-inflation environments. A company can raise prices to offset inflation. A fixed-rate bond has no such recourse to compensate investors.

Are bonds less risky than shares? They are less volatile, yet bonds can be a risk to achieving your goals if you can't earn a high enough return. The risk of inflation is also much higher with a bond. Do bonds belong in your portfolio? That's for you to decide, but it is worth considering the trade-off.

Does lowering volatility matter?

It may matter based on your specific goal. For instance, during the transition to retirement lowering volatility can be an important way to combat sequencing risk. It also matters because volatility causes investors to make poor decisions.

There are a few important points here:

1. Volatility is not how most investors should think about risk over the long term. The real risk is not earning high enough real (after inflation) returns to meet your goal.
2. The trade-off for lowering volatility is meaningfully lowering long-term returns. This significantly impacts the risk of not achieving your goal.
3. Bonds lower volatility but have significantly higher inflation risk when compared to shares. The risk of inflation destroying the purchasing power of your portfolio is one of the biggest you face as an investor.
4. While volatility is not a risk most long-term investors face, it does cause most people to make more bad decisions. That impacts long-term returns and puts your goals at risk.

(continued)

This is the conundrum we face as investors. Is there a way to lower our chances of making bad decisions while minimising the trade-off of lower returns putting our goal at risk?

In my own portfolio, I think I found a way to do this.

Bonds lower volatility but they don't eliminate it. They still exhibit volatility. Just less than shares. Sometimes bonds are negatively correlated to shares, meaning their prices move in the opposite direction to share prices. Sometimes they are positively correlated, which means they move in the same direction. It all depends on the economic environment.

But bonds still go down in price. The one asset that has no volatility is cash. If you put $100 in the bank it will be there when you want to get it out. And it will grow, although the growth will be less than bonds. Over the past 30 years (at 2024), cash has delivered returns of 4.2 per cent a year according to Vanguard. That's less than the 5.60 per cent from Australian bonds.

Like bonds, inflation is a large risk to holding cash. It may not have volatility but the money you put in the bank will also lose purchasing power over time. Over the past 30 years cash has delivered real returns of 1.50 per cent a year compared to 2.90 per cent for bonds.

While inflation is a risk to achieving my goals, and inflation is an outsized risk to both bonds and cash, I think cash is preferrable in a period of high inflation. Higher inflation and higher interest rates cause bond prices to drop. Cash held in a savings account or shorter-term term deposit does not fall in value and adjusts to the higher interest rates more quickly.

I could buy shorter-term bonds either individually or in an ETF. However, in an upward-sloping yield curve where longer-term bonds earn higher returns, I wouldn't get Vanguard's long-term bond returns without them. I just don't think the trade-off is worth it.

The beauty of cash is that to reduce the volatility of your portfolio by the same amount as holding bonds, you need less of it. That means you can hold more higher-returning shares. And if, like me, you've decided that volatility is not a risk you face as a long-term investor, cash may help to reduce the poor decisions you make by providing safety.

As I have got older I've grown the amount of cash I hold. It's nothing outrageous in the context of my overall assets, but it is meaningful when compared to my income. It helps me sleep well at night. Call it an emergency fund. Call it a strategic allocation to cash. Whatever, it gives me comfort, which I think makes it less likely fear will influence my decision making. It certainly worked during the COVID market drop.

This works for me. I'm not suggesting everyone should follow my approach. I do recommend spending some time thinking about if the investment industry's definition of risk is the one you face, and think about how to limit the impact of poor decisions on your portfolio.

Every investor can benefit from having clearly defined goals and an investment strategy that governs when changes are made to your portfolio. That is the premise of this book. In my case I think cash further insulates me from fear that leads to poor decision making.

I don't think most of the investors in the balanced option of super funds have thought about the trade-offs they are making. They picked balanced because they equated it with a personality trait that sounds positive. Who doesn't want to be known as balanced? Whatever the reason, I'm positive that

(continued)

a balanced portfolio won't answer the needs of many of the Australians who are currently invested in it.

More than anything, this is a call to think about the approach you're taking with your finances. Interrogate the conventional wisdom and the actions of professional investment managers. It doesn't mean they're wrong. But they might not be right for your personal circumstances.

Exercise: A checklist for evaluating investments

In this exercise you get to practise evaluating investments. If you're already an investor, the best place to practise is on investments you already own. Going through the process of defining your investment philosophy, your goals and your investment strategy may have caused you to question certain of your holdings. Perhaps you no longer think they are the right investments to help you achieve your goals. Time to put them through their paces.

At this point you should have defined a set of criteria for evaluating investments. Those criteria will be unique to your investment goals and strategy. However, we believe there are some things that every investor should consider when selecting an investment.

A key message throughout this book is to add structure to your decision making. A checklist is a good way of doing that. This checklist contains some general questions that would apply to any investment and some specific questions if you are investing in individual shares or a fund or ETF. Document and save these checklists for each investment you buy. They will come in handy when you do portfolio reviews or you are considering selling an investment and want to re-evaluate your thesis.

We know the concept of a checklist seems simplistic. We know it is hard to imagine an investing savant following a checklist. But lots of highly trained and highly intelligent people follow checklists. When you are sitting on a plane waiting for it to push back from the gate the pilot is going through a checklist. If you are having an operation the surgeon is going through a checklist. It is a simple and effective way of improving your decision making.

This checklist is not intended as an exhaustive list of how to research a share, fund or ETF. It simply identifies some high-level questions that you should be able to answer about any investment you are considering. If you can't answer these questions, you might be making a decision influenced by the opinion of a friend, a commentator or marketing from the investment industry.

General questions

1. How does this investment help me achieve my goal?
2. What is my thesis for making this investment? Why will my desired outcome occur?
3. Why won't my desired outcome occur?
4. What emotions may be influencing my decision to buy this investment? Without those emotions would I make a different decision?

Share questions

1. Why do customers buy a product/service from this company?
2. What are the main criteria influencing a customer's decision to buy a product/service from this company?

(continued)

3. What are the alternatives to buying a product/service from this company? Who offers similar products/services and what are the substitutes (including not purchasing at all)?

4. Will revenue/sales grow in the future and by how much? How big is the overall opportunity for the company? What factors will influence revenue growth?

5. How much of the revenue will the company get to keep as profits? What factors will influence this amount?

6. If this company succeeds, how will competitors respond and what prevents them from creating a better product/service or selling a similar product/service for less?

7. Given the three sources of return – dividends, valuation changes and earnings growth – where would future returns come from? What has driven returns in the past?

ETF/fund questions

1. What investment exposure does this ETF/fund provide and why do I want exposure to this type of investment?

2. How does the ETF/fund select individual securities? Does a human make the decision, and if so what do I know about the investment selection process? If the ETF/fund is passive, what are the index criteria used for identifying investments?

3. How often and what criteria are used to change the holdings in the ETF/fund?

4. What weighting criteria are used to determine position sizing in the ETF/fund?

5. What are the main drivers for performance of this ETF/fund? Are there certain conditions under which this ETF will perform well or poorly? How has it performed in the past in different conditions?

Key takeaways

While there are many investing strategies and lots of different ways to evaluate a potential investment, there are some time-tested foundational elements to how the market works. Returns come from only three places: dividends, changes in valuation levels and earnings growth. Each company and investment is different, which makes it critical to figure out which ones are right for you.

A great place to practise evaluating different investment opportunities is with the shares, funds and ETFs you already own. Like everything else, this involves practice. Apply your criteria to your current holdings. Our generic checklist will start you on the process of building a portfolio designed specifically to achieve your goals.

When a house is more than a home

Warren Buffett was 25 years old when he moved from New York to Omaha in 1956. He had two children and for the time a sizable nest egg of $127000. He could have bought a house without a mortgage for about a quarter of his net worth. What did Buffett do? He rented a house for $175 a month.

His rationale for not buying a house says a lot about who he is as a person. As Buffett relayed in an article for *Forbes*, he told his wife, 'I'd be glad to buy a house, but that's like a carpenter selling his toolkit.' He thought he would be better off if he invested the money instead.

The lesson from this story is not that you avoid buying a house. Buffett relented two years later and purchased the house he still lives in for $31000. The lesson is to think about your financial resources and the best use for them. Buffett thought the best use for his money was to invest it. Of course you likely aren't Warren Buffett. Neither are we.

The best use for your financial resources isn't just measured in dollars and cents. It's also measured in happiness and satisfaction in life. That makes housing tricky. On the one hand, owning your home fulfils an innate need for stability and security while allowing you to design a place to live that suits your needs. On the other hand, there are lots of reasons why owning a home helps to increase wealth, including generous tax breaks, the impact of the leverage of a mortgage on building wealth and the forced savings of paying back the principal on your mortgage. Then there is the fact that historically house prices in Australia have gone up. A lot.

This combination of the emotional and financial factors wrapped up in housing makes it very difficult to make a rational decision. It's just too easy to justify stretching for a home you might not be able to afford. So be careful.

Property versus shares

Property has made a lot of Australians wealthy. We understand why many are drawn to the idea of property as an investment. Before exploring the pros and cons of property and shares we need to provide a warning and some perspective.

Much of the budgeting advice we hear addresses small expenses. Bring your lunch to work and make coffee at home are just a few of the common money saving tips. Small expenses add up, and there's nothing wrong with this advice, except that much of it misses the point. What will have the biggest influence on the type of life you live and your financial situation is the big purchases. And there's no bigger expense than where you live.

If you buy a house you can't afford, or if you can't afford your rent, there are no tricks to get yourself out of the situation. You will have a very difficult time trying to achieve financial freedom under these circumstances.

The issue isn't just paying the mortgage or the rent. If your rent or mortgage takes up too large a percentage of your income, you are constantly on the edge of financial instability. Any increase in interest rates or rent could push you over the edge. Higher monthly housing costs mean you need a bigger emergency fund to protect you if anything goes wrong, which means less money to invest. A more expensive house has higher maintenance and upkeep costs. Many people stretch when it comes to housing. There's an emotional aspect that makes it easy to spend too much, and there are simple justifications, such as the 'inevitability' of earning more money in the future. Be very careful about these decisions, and keep in mind that the larger the expense, the more time you should spend thinking it through. The decision on whether to buy your coffee or to make your own is not a big deal. Where you live and what kind of car you drive matter far more.

The other way many people justify buying a house they can't afford is to say it's an investment. We think this is also dangerous. The assumption is that the houses that previous generations of Australians have purchased have appreciated so there will be continued appreciation in the future. Maybe or maybe not. But it's important to recognise that many of the people who have seen their house appreciate over the years didn't buy it as an investment. These gains were unintentional, as they purchased their home as a place to live, not as a pathway to riches.

Investment property

Purchasing a home to live in has very different considerations from an investment. Buying a home is a financial goal, so it's not an asset. You won't realise any capital growth until you sell, at which time you will have to find somewhere else to live. When purchasing a home, there are lots of considerations, mostly around the home you want to live in. The potential yield, the industries in the area and assessing the tax benefits are not front of mind.

Purchasing a property as an investment requires you to consider cash flows, maintenance and upkeep costs, and demand and supply of property in the area. Evaluating an investment property is very different from choosing a home. Remember that as investment vehicles property and shares are not mutually exclusive. Many people choose to do both.

The issue with property in Australia now is that it's expensive, which has implications as investment properties are generally cash-flow negative. This can be offset by negative gearing, which is a tax break that counteracts the impact of the investment property costing an investor more in mortgage payments, maintenance costs, depreciation and other costs than the cash collected in rent.

For a new investment property to be a successful investment, the property must appreciate. Remember, if all your funds are locked up in an investment property, you are not diversified. Local conditions and property-specific conditions will drive your return.

Paying off your mortgage or investing

We're often asked whether it makes better sense to direct any extra cash to paying off a mortgage or to investing. The answer depends on your personal circumstances, but we provide a framework for making a decision.

The best decision will come down to the returns of any money invested. Since future returns are unknowable, the best approach is to calculate a hurdle rate. A hurdle rate is the benchmark return that needs to be exceeded to make it worthwhile to invest instead of paying down your mortgage.

Let's have a look at an example.

Imagine you've purchased a $1 million house with a $200 000 deposit, a 6 per cent interest rate and property appreciation of 7.1 per cent annually over 11 years. Eleven years is the average time an Aussie holds onto a house. For the purposes of this example, we've ignored costs such as stamp duty and maintenance/upkeep.

By the end of that period, your property would be worth $2.1 million. After paying down part of your loan, you'd walk away with $1.451 million (table 11.1). Although impressive, let's take a look at the costs: $481k goes towards interest, with only $146k going to the principal. Interest is a huge cost for property investors and is the initial hurdle rate for investors.

Table 11.1: cost of purchasing a property

Category	Amount ($)
Deposit	200 000
Principal payments	146 857
Interest payments	481 471
Loan balance at sale	653 142
Sale price	2 104 851
Owner proceeds/total wealth	1 451 709

Now let's look at prepayments. Let's say you decided to pay an extra $1000 a month towards the mortgage. That simple change would shorten the loan term and significantly reduce interest costs (table 11.2). Over the same 11 years, you'd save $53 000 in interest and increase the amount of principal you'd paid by $132 000. Your total wealth would rise to $1.636 million — $184 000 more than if you'd just stuck to the standard mortgage payments. These are non-compulsory payments towards your mortgage that could have been redirected to other assets.

We need to make some adjustments prior to calculating a hurdle rate. It's important that you include all costs associated with investing, and this includes tax. Paying off a mortgage is tax-free, but investments are not. Any dividends earned or capital gains realised from shares would be subject to taxes. This makes the hurdle rate even higher. For example, those in the 37 per cent tax bracket would need to earn 7.8 per cent, and those in the 45 per cent tax bracket would have to earn 8.3 per cent to make investing worthwhile. Tax is a huge cost for investors.

Table 11.2: impact of extra repayments on cost of purchasing a house

Category	Amount ($)
Deposit	200 000
Principal payments	331 258
Interest payments	428 070
Loan balance at sale	468 741
Sale price	2 104 851
Owner proceeds/total wealth	1 636 110

This improves if you're investing in a tax-effective vehicle (table 11.3) such as superannuation.

Table 11.3: investing in a taxable account

Marginal tax rate (%)	Hurdle rate (%)
30	7.50
37	7.80
45	8.30

By making concessional contributions, you're able to lower the tax liability and the hurdle rate significantly (table 11.4). For someone in the 45 per cent tax bracket, the effective hurdle rate could even become negative. Super contributions are almost guaranteed to outperform mortgage prepayments in those cases. Of course, there are limits to the amount of concessional contributions that can be contributed. Regardless, it is a powerful tool for investors.

Morningstar has 5-, 10- and 15-year projections for asset classes. These are projected rather than historical returns. These are the same projected returns we referenced earlier in the book. They take into consideration the current market and economic conditions and a forecast for the likely future outcomes. Projected returns offer investors the opportunity to make more informed decisions about their future outcomes than historical returns would and are an interesting comparison to the hurdle rates above (table 11.5, overleaf).

Table 11.4: concessional superannuation contributions with same pre-tax amount

Marginal tax rate (%)	Hurdle rate (%)
30	3.20
37	1.90
45	−0.66

Table 11.5: asset class long-term (20 years) return assumptions

Asset classes	Expected return (% p.a.)
Australian equity*	7.90
International equity (45% hedged)	6.75
Australian listed property	6.85
International listed property	7.00
Australian fixed interest	2.00
International fixed interest	2.25
Cash	1.75

Source: Morningstar 2024.
*Return expectations for Australian equities incorporate franking credits.

We're long-term investors. It's important to look at a scenario where you hold the house for longer than the average of 11 years. If you keep it for 30 years and continue to prepay $1000 monthly, the mortgage could be paid off in 20 years instead of 30. This would save $465 000 in interest and give 10 years of mortgage-free cash flows to invest or use as you see fit. The trade-off here of paying off your mortgage and then investing (sequentially) instead of investing and paying your mortgage (concurrently) is that you do miss out on the 20 years of compounding returns from equity investments.

This book is dedicated to helping you achieve financial freedom. Paying off your mortgage is a great step in that direction. It's most people's largest expense and not having to pay provides you with a lot of options. You can spend or invest the money that was going to your mortgage. You could work less since you've eliminated such a large expense. The issue with paying off your mortgage is that you don't get any benefit from paying off 90 per cent of your mortgage. You must make that last payment to realise the benefit. Think about how to get there and understand that borrowing more money on your house moves you further away from your goal.

There are pros and cons to deciding to pay off your mortgage or investing any extra funds. Understanding what your hurdle rate is will give you a basis for a more informed decision. If you can earn higher returns than the hurdle rate, investing may be the logical choice. It means you have balanced your investments across different asset classes, you've mitigated risk, and you've maintained flexibility through liquidity. However, if a guaranteed outcome suits your temperament better, prepaying your mortgage offers financial security and peace of mind.

Exercise: Evaluate the role of property in your financial life

For many Australians their primary place of residence is their biggest asset and largest expense. It's hard to come up with a plan to achieve financial independence without housing playing a large role. We understand there are also lots of emotional components to housing. For now, we are asking you to put those aside.

There are several questions we think it's helpful to answer about the role housing plays in your finances:

1. What trade-offs are you making by owning a home or not owning a home? How do these trade-offs compare to what you want in life?

2. If you own your home, in what way will it support achieving what you want out of life? Is it through price appreciation and selling your home later in life to downsize or move to a cheaper location? Is it through paying off your mortgage, removing a large expense from your budget?

3. What assumptions are you making with regard to housing, and what happens to your financial future if those assumptions don't play out the way you anticipate? These

(continued)

assumptions may include levels of interest rates, future price appreciation matching past performance or any other factor related to your unique situation.

This exercise should give you more insight into how you view housing. That is always helpful, even though most people are unlikely to make a radical change in their view on housing. However, especially if you are saving for a home, it is worth considering what you are giving up based on the high price of real estate in Australia.

Shani never thought she would own a home ... until she did

One (wonderful) complication to financial goals is having someone else to consider. When I married Matt we came into the relationship with two very different upbringings, two different financial perspectives and two sets of goals.

One of the decisions that I made very early on was that I wasn't going to sacrifice my lifestyle to purchase a house. I had spent my childhood and most of my adult life commuting. I grew up in Quakers Hill, and getting to Sydney city and back required me to travel for at least two and a half hours a day door to door. With the hours I was working, I barely saw family or friends, and when I did I was exhausted.

Some people are happy with this trade-off, and I respect their view and understand the motivations for wanting to build a sense of security by owning a home. It wasn't that I didn't want a house. I just didn't think owning a home was worth it. The decision I made was based purely on my limited resources and appreciation of the trade-offs I would have to make. Not only would I be sacrificing on lifestyle, but I would likely be sacrificing on something that brings me a great amount of joy, and that is travel. Growing up, all of my travel was to Sri Lanka. I'm very lucky to be connected to such a beautiful place. However, I wanted to see more of the world and build my financial security in other assets — namely, equities.

One of my husband's main financial goals was to own a home. Not as an investment, not for capital growth, not to sell later and scoop the cream off the top for further financial security. It was to have a home, to have a permanent place where we could start our lives with a sense of emotional security.

I was happy with this financial goal as long as it did not impede my other financial goals. It's extremely difficult to purchase a home in Australia, let alone in Sydney, without making sacrifices. We are a dual income household on good salaries with no dependants or caring responsibilities. Our student loans were paid off. We were able to opt for Land Tax instead of Stamp Duty. It required all of the stars to align perfectly and a lot of hard work. Matt contributed more to the deposit, as this was a longstanding goal of his.

This significantly altered my financial considerations. I now hold a lot of debt and an asset that is growing in value, but value I won't realise as I have no interest in selling it.

Like many other instances in life, you don't know how you're going to react to a situation until you're in it. I have always had an aversion to debt. It goes against the financial security that is paramount for me and my goals. I couldn't rationalise away this feeling by classifying my giant mortgage as 'good debt'. I still struggle not to put all my other financial goals on hold and pay down the debt as quickly as possible.

This is a strategy that works for a lot of people, but I have a solid financial plan that gives me the best chance of achieving all my important financial goals within the capacity and constraints I have.

Mark's perspective on property

Owning your own home is more than a financial decision. To start with, I want to make it clear that I feel no emotional attachment to property. I have never thought that owning a home was an important life stage and I've never cared if anyone thought less of me for not owning a home. I know this isn't the case for a lot of people. What matters to me is where I live. I want to walk to work, and I want a neighbourhood that's filled with bars and restaurants and is close to public transportation because I don't want to own a car. I also want as much of my income as possible to be available for discretionary spending. Currently I rent in Surry Hills, a popular inner-city suburb of Sydney, and I pay approximately 7 per cent of my combined household income on rent. I don't see a scenario where I would buy a place in the near term given the prices in inner-city suburbs.

The second lens through which we can view property is as an investment. I have owned investment properties in the US. Before getting into them, it's important to connect investment property to my investment approach. My goal for my non-retirement accounts is to generate income, which means I'm primarily interested in cash flow. I care about generating as much cash flow as possible and I use it for discretionary spending. I want to pay for experiences. To travel, to go out to eat — to pay for things I enjoy. My primary concern for all my investments including property isn't capital growth. Obviously I would like the investment properties I own to go up in value, but that didn't factor into my decision making. My motivation and criteria to pick properties were their ability to generate cash flow.

When it comes to cash flow, there are two different factors I consider for investment properties. The first is the set monthly cost — the mortgage. It was important to me that the mortgage costs were fixed over the life of a 30-year loan. This is easy in the US as a 30-year fixed-rate mortgage is standard. For every property I have, I will know what I am paying every month for the life of the loan. The variable costs like the insurance and property tax may increase, but most of the cost is fixed.

This is difficult to do in Australia, where the fixed portion of your mortgage is shorter term. It's important to model out scenarios. We've seen historically low interest rates in the recent past and this has tripped up many investors. The speed of rate increases was unprecedented. However, what everyone was calling high interest rates were actually about average historically.

If I was investing for capital appreciation, I would think about what impact a rising interest rate would have on property prices. Generally, the direction of prices would be downward. If I was investing for cash flow, I would think about my ability to pass on those higher costs in higher rents.

When I purchased properties they were already rented out, so I was confident that the rent levels represented market pricing. I was also confident that rents would increase over time. This has a lot to do with the communities I picked out. Increasing rent is very much a product of local economic conditions. I bought properties that were close to large universities because they would maintain the local economy in all economic conditions. I also bought in a town that had a large and growing Mercedes plant in Alabama, as I thought this offered some protection. The local community is an important factor for those who want to generate income and those who want capital appreciation.

When deciding what a fair price to pay was I used the cash flow yield. I knew the costs, the rent and an estimate for non-standard costs. I wanted an annual cash flow yield of 10 per cent on my deposit.

(continued)

For Australians, this situation is near impossible. Property prices in the US are cheap for the most part when you get out of major coastal cities and their suburbs. This is where I went because there was attractive cash flow yield, and I could buy multiple properties for diversification.

In Australia you need a lot of cash to build a diversified property portfolio. The inherent issue with purchasing a property is that things can and will go wrong. You may not have a tenant. There may be structural repairs. You may pick a bad place to buy. You can reduce the risk of this happening, but it can't be eliminated. The biggest risk we can make with any investment is to project current conditions into the future.

Cities fall into and out of favour. People stretching for investment property often go and buy wherever they can, and that can lead to problems. If you buy in the wrong location, even within a town or city, you may be faced with declining rents and declining housing prices. I own one property that has been a disaster from day one. I had a tenant who stopped paying rent and I had to hire a lawyer to process an eviction. He didn't vacate the property, and the property management company weren't aware of it. Even though there was no electricity, he still lived there, and I had to get the Sheriff to show up and forcibly evict him. You can imagine the state of the place when he left. I had to pay to get it back into shape. This place has had long periods of vacancy; a tree fell on it, and the last tenant actually put the iron on the floor and burned an iron-shaped hole in the carpet.

All of these issues are property-specific as opposed to systemic risk, which for property could be interest rate levels, population changes in a certain area and the overall economy. When we build a portfolio, we diversify away company-specific risk by owning multiple holdings. The issue with Australian property investment is that property-specific risks can't always be diversified away because housing is so expensive.

Inherent with property investment is debt, and this is where it comes back to me. I'm just not comfortable holding large amounts of debt. Leverage increases the risk of any investment. You get a higher upside and a higher downside. Over time, as you pay down your mortgage, you remove leverage, which mathematically lowers the upside of your house. I think this is underappreciated.

Many people choose to take equity out of their investment properties and reinvest it in other properties. I'm too conservative for this approach. I'm uncomfortable with debt. Borrowing and investing money works really well, until it doesn't.

Some investors take out interest-only mortgages. This will minimise your repayment, which will increase your cash flow. The downside is that you aren't building up any equity. I think this approach is fairly attractive from the perspective of price appreciation. You just better be right about the direction the market is going. You have more risk if prices fall because there's no equity in the house. Personally, I'm too cautious for that approach.

There are many ways that property can be used by investors in their portfolio. I'm lucky that I can leverage cheaper housing prices and 30-year fixed-term mortgages in the US. Being able to spread my risk across several properties makes this an attractive investment from a cash flow perspective because I've lowered concentration risk. I'm not sure that this strategy is possible in Australia given the cost of housing and the inability to lock in a mortgage rate for the

(continued)

life of the loan. There are, of course, many attractive aspects to Australian property that make it worthwhile for investors, including the generous tax breaks. Still, my preference for positive cash flows and my aversion to debt mean I choose not to participate in the Australian housing market, either with a primary place of residence or as an investment. This is just a case of investing my way and keeping my goals in mind.

Key takeaways

Purchasing a house involves an emotional pull and a narrative that housing is a great way to build wealth. That combination can cause investors to stretch for housing. Look at housing within the framework of your overall goals to ensure you are directing your financial resources to a place that adds most to your life.

By documenting how housing fits into your financial plan and goals, you can get a better sense of whether your decisions are aligned with what you want out of life. Also, by thinking through the assumptions you've made about how property will support your financial goals, you can anticipate the consequences if those assumptions don't play out. This will give you a clearer perspective on the financial choices you are making.

Stay on the pathway to financial freedom

Have you heard of Sylvia Bloom? How about Grace Groner? Or maybe Ronald Read? Probably not. These unassuming people were little known during their lifetimes, but on their death each was discovered to have amassed a great fortune. They had one other thing in common: they were all long-term investors who stuck primarily to a buy-and-hold strategy. They also all kept the fact that they were investors — and good at it — a secret.

Maybe their reticence was the secret to their success. They weren't trying to project their success, and they didn't have to live up to the expectations of others. They were able to tune out all the noise and just focus on the long term.

We've laid out a framework for financial freedom. This framework focuses on ensuring that you have the foundations for success and that you build your portfolio around your circumstances and goals. If you've gone through the steps we've outlined, you have a plan — and that's a great start. We hope you also have greater self-awareness of the type of life you want to live and how your finances can help you get there. We hope you have a set of goals and an investment strategy designed to achieve them. Now you just need to follow the plan.

The purpose of establishing a framework to help govern your decision making is to improve your behaviour. We've talked about this book's focus on leveraging two types of edge — structural and behavioural. A common theme has been that investors self-sabotage by following conventional wisdom and letting emotions play too big a role in day-to-day money decisions. To end the book, we want to offer guidance on some common decisions that will help you stay on the pathway to financial freedom.

Mark says ...

Investors are commonly advised against checking their portfolio too often. I agree with that advice, and I know that is the approach that Shani takes. I admire her for that and think she is doing the right thing. In saying that, I also admit that I check my portfolio frequently. Not every day but usually at least once a week. What helps me is that I have context when I check my portfolio. I don't just look at what has gone up and what has gone down. I look at how I'm tracking towards my goals. Without context it becomes too easy to make decisions based on nothing more than short-term performance. That's a trap too many investors fall into.

Monitoring your progress towards your goal

One of the most challenging aspects of investing is you are constantly getting feedback on your investments. When markets are open prices go up and down minute by minute. Everyone, from friends and family to market commentators to complete strangers, weigh in on what is a good investment and what isn't. Everyone has an opinion on what you should do with your money.

Ironically the signals from the market, many of the people that give you advice and your own emotions tell you to do exactly the opposite of what you should do. When the market goes up everyone — and your own intuition — thinks the market is safer and there's less risk of a downturn. Actually the risk is higher. Conversely when the market falls, it seems riskier. It isn't.

To understand why means going back to the point we made earlier on expectations. When prices go up, investor expectations for the future are higher, but it's harder to meet those higher expectations. When markets fall, expectations are lower. In the depths of a bear market, despair sets in, yet exceeding these low expectations is relatively easy to do.

We can see this impact when we look at returns at different valuation levels. Researchers from Morningstar Investment Management conducted a study on how valuations can impact your returns. The higher the valuation levels, the lower the future returns.

Logically, we know this is the case. We know that investing in overpriced assets means more risk is involved. This study shows empirically the opportunity cost of chasing returns and investing in overpriced assets. The Morningstar study looked at the investable universe in 24 countries, sorting it into three portfolio buckets based on valuation.

The three valuation buckets were created using our price to fair value estimate, which is our view of how much a share is worth. The shares were sorted into the cheapest bucket, a middle bucket and the most overvalued bucket. These buckets were re-sorted monthly between 1975 and 2016 based on changes in valuation.

The results look at the growth of a dollar. Let's start with the most overvalued bucket. Over 40 years you earned more than five times your money and end up with $5.19. Not all that attractive but positive. Then there's the middle bucket, where the $1 turned into $14.77. Much better. The last bucket of the cheapest shares turned into $100.89. That's over 100 times your money.

Having a goal can signal the right behaviour during volatile markets

It is easy for us to tell you not to react to market movements. It is easy for us to insist that successful investing is buying low and selling high. Most investors know that, and most investors still pile in at the top of the market and sell at the bottom.

One reason for going through the goal-setting process is to help you avoid this mistake. If you've gone through the process, then you have a required rate of return. The required rate of return will signal clearly what you should do.

We will use a scenario in which an investor has $100 000 invested and will be saving $10 000 a year. To hit the goal of $800 000, the required rate of return is 7 per cent over the next 20 years.

For five years returns are great. Despite needing only a 7 per cent return the portfolio goes up 12 per cent a year. The $100 000 portfolio grows to $240 000 including the additional savings. After five years of high returns most investors become confident that those returns will continue. Logically this is the wrong reaction. If returns are above average for a while, they need to be below average for a while to even things out. But that isn't how most people think.

Humans are afflicted with recency bias, which means we give greater importance to recent events than historic events and expect things to continue the same way they've been going. That's why people tend to pile into the sharemarket when it has been on a strong run. The longer the run lasts the more confident people are that it will continue. New investors and investing sceptics tend to get in at the end of a bull market, just in time to get burned. Many give up and never return.

We want to prevent that behaviour. A core part of monitoring your portfolio is to recalculate the required rate of return. We can turn back to our earlier example where the portfolio grew by 12 per cent a year over the first five years. If the other assumptions remain the same and only the time to the goal and the portfolio balance change, the required rate of return when recalculated is 5.90 per cent. It has dropped from 7 per cent because of the strong run of 12 per cent annual returns.

As we outlined in the goal-setting process, the return you need to achieve is the primary driver of how you invest. This impacts the asset allocation between defensive assets and growth assets. A lower required rate of return would signal a more conservative asset allocation.

Time for several caveats. We don't think you should adjust your asset allocation with every change of a required rate of return. This is market timing. However, the critical point here is that the signal you are getting from looking at the required rate of return is the opposite one you are getting from your friends and family, the media and your intuition. The required rate of return is telling you that you don't have to take more risk to achieve your goal. Everyone else is telling you to put more money into the market to take advantage of a future that will look like the recent past.

The same thing happens if the market drops or if returns are lower than what you need to achieve your goal. The required rate of return goes up, which is a signal that you need to stay invested in growth assets to achieve a higher return. Knowing this helps signal that you shouldn't sell low, at the bottom of the market.

This is yet another example of using structure to prevent poor decisions. Nobody is perfect and every investor is going to make mistakes. The emotional pull to do the wrong thing is just too strong. The goal is to reduce mistakes. Using this approach for monitoring a portfolio is far more likely to reduce mistakes than what most investors do, which is to look at what went up and what went down.and make decisions based on that.

Calculating a required rate of return also provides a benchmark that can be used to judge how your portfolio is doing. Professional investors and some individual investors use a benchmark to judge performance. They will see if their portfolio has outperformed or underperformed an index. Yet for many investors with diversified portfolios, it is difficult to come up with an appropriate index. Performance against an index is fairly meaningless because it won't tell you if you are on track to achieve your goals. If you need a 7 per cent return and achieve an 8 per cent return, you know that this year was a good one and you got closer to your goal. Relative performance against a benchmark doesn't tell you any of that.

How often you should check your portfolio

The last question is how often you should check your portfolio. We think you should do an in-depth review at least once a year but no more than every six months, which includes recalculating your required rate of return, comparing your asset allocation to your target asset allocation and ensuring you are properly diversified. This is also a good time to see if you are meeting your savings goals.

We know you are going to check your portfolio more often. Try to resist the urge, because checking too much makes it more likely that you will adjust your portfolio. We've outlined multiple times why this is a mistake. One bonus of checking your portfolio less frequently is that it might make you happier. We humans suffer from something called loss aversion, which basically means the emotional impact of a loss is greater than the joy of an equivalent gain.

The S&P 500 has had a positive return in a day 53.70 per cent of the time since 1951. Over a year, however, the return has been positive 73 per cent of the time. If you look at your portfolio daily, 46 per cent of the time you will see a loss, which makes you more unhappy than the days it has gone up. If you check only once a year, there's less chance you will be unhappy.

Shani says ...

It seems only logical that the amount you monitor your portfolio should match the time horizon for reaching your goals. Many investors get bogged down in reading the news, interpreting its impact on their portfolio and calculating how to position it for the best success. The daily movements of markets and the swings of individual companies should not require close attention when you're planning on achieving your goal in the distant future. It breeds poor behaviour. My portfolio is like a plant that thrives on neglect. I monitor my portfolio at set intervals — every six months — to determine whether I'm still on track for my goals. When major market movements or events happen, I check in. My portfolio is a means to an end; it's not a job in and of itself.

Reviewing individual positions in your portfolio

We've repeatedly advised investors to trade less and showed numerous examples of how constantly buying and selling investments prevents investors from achieving their goals. When reviewing your portfolio, it is inevitable that you will look at the relative performance of individual holdings, and you will be tempted to sell the holdings that aren't doing well.

The downsides of selling are considerable. The first is tax. We can use an example to illustrate the impact that taxes have on returns. If an investor is fortunate enough to buy a company that has doubled in price, we can explore the tax consequences of selling.

Purchasing a share for $1000 and selling it for $2000 with a holding period of less than a year at a 37 per cent marginal tax rate results in capital gains of $370. That would require the new investment opportunity to outperform the sold share by 18.5 per cent just to break even, assuming the taxes are paid separately. If the taxes are paid out of the gains and only $1630 is reinvested, the return would have to be 22.69 per cent to break even.

If the same scenario is run with the long-term capital gains discount applied to shares held for more than a year, the taxes would be $185. In that case it would require the new investment opportunity to outperform the sold share by 9.25 per cent to break even, assuming the taxes are paid separately. If the taxes are paid out of the gains and only $1815 is invested, the return would have to be 10.19 per cent to break even.

That's a high hurdle rate, and it doesn't include any transaction costs associated with the trades. There are other reasons not to sell. As investors we want to truly understand the businesses we own. The more we understand a business, the less likely we will panic and sell when the price plunges in an irrational way. Longer holding periods gives an investor an opportunity to truly understand a business.

There are downsides to this of course. Investors can form attachments to certain positions. Being a good investor means remaining as rational as possible while acknowledging that complete rationality is impossible. Forming an attachment to a share is irrational. However, when combined with a clearly defined investment strategy, a long-holding period is a more reasonable approach than the trap of constantly churning a portfolio that many investors fall into.

Warren Buffett famously said his favourite holding period is forever. We think the best approach is to set a high bar for selling a position. This doesn't mean you won't ever sell anything. It does mean that you will think long and hard before doing so. This is how you can prevent yourself from falling into the trap of overtrading.

Exercise: Monitoring your portfolio

If you have completed each of the exercises in this book, you now have structure around your decision making. You've also evaluated some of your current holdings against your goals. It's now time to take a step back and look at your overall portfolio. Answer the following questions based on the different exercises you've done throughout this book:

1. *How is my portfolio performing against my required rate of return?* Go back in time with your account statements and the goal you defined, and calculate the required rate of return at different points in the past. This will show the

(continued)

impact of returns and savings on your overall progress towards your goal. Has that required rate of return gone up or down over the past few years?

2. *How are my savings levels compared to what I've used in my goal assumptions?* Have you saved too little or too much in the past. How can you make changes to savings levels in the future to ensure you stay on track to achieve your goals.

These are both simple checks. The combination of returns and savings is the key to achieving your goals.

Shani walks the tightrope between efficiency and maximising outcomes

Part of reviewing your portfolio is acknowledging that the markets change, but so do the investment product options available to you as an investor. When reviewing your portfolio to understand whether the products you are in are still the best to achieve your outcomes, you must also weigh up the costs of switching.

I use managed funds in my portfolio. I started using managed funds at the beginning of my investing journey. At the time I was earning $56 000 a year and living out of home in Sydney. This was very challenging for me financially. I had student loans with compulsory payments, and I had very little discretionary spending or room for saving. Most weeks I was able to put aside only $50 to $100. I had only one viable option for investing these small amounts. The ETF industry in Australia was then comparatively embryonic. Brokerage was more expensive, and fees weren't as low as they are now.

Managed funds offered me a way into the market. They allowed me to start investing my money immediately, to build discipline and to invest much earlier than other options because of the low barriers for additional investments.

Of course my situation has changed. I earn more, and I have more left over to invest. I have the ability to consider other options outside managed funds. I can invest in larger parcels with listed assets – and I do. I invest in ETFs. In chapter 9 I laid out my investment strategy. I explained that at its core it is about controlling what I can control, limiting costs like fees and taxes, reducing poor behaviour and investing as much as I can in the market. Most of these goals can be fulfilled with ETFs.

I believe fees are important. ETFs typically have lower fees. I believe minimising tax costs is important. ETFs generally are better than managed funds in this respect.

This is where investors must walk a tightrope. It's important to be efficient with your investments, but not to the detriment of your total return outcomes.

The industry will always be innovating. There will always be new investment products and options for investors to choose from. Choosing a marginally better option each and every time one appears will not improve your outcomes. You'll incur tax on sale (if you've made a profit) and transaction costs. Investors know in principle not to chase returns and switch in and out of products. There should be a logical and sensible reason why you decide to switch out of an investment product with a long-term plan. You will inevitably continue to see innovation as more investment product providers compete for your money.

I strongly believe that switching investments every time a new one appears – and incurring transaction fees and capital

(continued)

gains taxes — will put you in a far worse position. It is a balance, and I know that as my portfolio grows, the ratio of my assets in ETFs will increase.

It doesn't mean I'll sell my managed funds. They suit the other goals of my portfolio. They allow me to invest as much as I can in the market. The funds I have left over from my pay cheque go into my managed funds. This was the vehicle that helped me to start investing in the first place and now it ensures I maximise how much I am able to invest.

Managed funds may also be a good solution for investors who are prone to overtrading.

I would be the first to admit that I am a nervous investor. My anxiety about markets presents in an interesting way. When markets are down, I endeavour to follow my plan and get as much money invested as possible. When markets are up, however, it's more difficult for me, as I have to resist the urge to sell, to harvest my gains before potential impending doom. Funds limit this behaviour and help me stay invested over the long term.

How Mark's default prevents overtrading

Everything I've learned about markets and investor behaviour has led me to the conclusion that the biggest mistake the average investor can make is trading too much. To combat this, I've simply adopted a view that my default is not selling an investment, ever.

This has two impacts on my behaviour. The first is that I'm more careful about why I buy. If I'm never going to sell something, I need to be very sure that what I buy is right for me.

It also raises the bar extremely high for anything that I do sell. By seeing selling as an exception to the rule, I need to spend more time finding ways to justify my action.

There are obvious downsides to this. I've held onto positions for too long even after I've decided something in my original thesis was not playing out. This has cost me some money. Yet I think the benefits outweigh the costs, and I truly believe most investors would have better results if they simply cut back on trading.

I don't do a lot of things right in the way I monitor my portfolio. I check it often and I am probably too engaged with the investing news cycle, but that's mostly just my job. It is hard for me not to form opinions about what is going on in markets. Like everyone else, I get anxious over certain events. I worry about my choices and second-guess myself. I wish I could be more of an investing stoic. Yet I've reached a place where I don't act on my opinions or my emotions. I've got better at it over time, and I feel fortunate I've been able to achieve this. More than anything else, it will help me to achieve my goals.

Key takeaways

To ensure that you meet your financial goals, the work doesn't stop when you've chosen the investments for your investment portfolio. Markets, economic conditions and even your goals can change over long time horizons. Monitoring your portfolio allows you to make the necessary changes to stay on track. Your investment strategy is important in this process. It will ensure you have guidance for any changes in your portfolio and help prevent decisions triggered by emotions.

Now you have a plan, you can evaluate how you have done in the past against that plan. Most investors have little context when they are reviewing their finances. You now know the required rate of return and level of savings you need to achieve your goal. Keeping yourself on target using those two metrics will help you continue to progress towards financial independence.

Epilogue

We decided that this book would be different. Instead of focusing on how to find great investments, we would help you become a better investor. We wanted to challenge some of the stereotypes around what it takes to be a successful investor. We think these misconceptions about how to be successful cause many investors to sabotage their outcomes.

We've pointed to multiple studies showing how investor behaviour impacts outcomes. We want to leave you with one more. Dalbar's annual 'Quantitative Analysis of Investor Behavior' (QAIB) report measures investor returns. In a recent report looking at the average performance of individual investors in the US from 1998 through 2017, they estimated the average investor earned a return of 2.60 per cent. That is shockingly bad. Over the same period inflation was 2.10 per cent a year. Investors barely grew the purchasing power of their money. A passive portfolio made up of 60 per cent US shares and 40 per cent US bonds had a 6.40 per cent annual return.

If you want a different outcome then you need to do something different. Most people don't give much thought to their overall money philosophy. You have now interrogated your own money narrative. Most people don't bother to define their goals. You have.

Most people don't have a personalised investment strategy, so they pinball back and forth among trendy investments. You now have a plan and the structure to improve your decision making.

We've illustrated how the only thing holding investors back is their own poor behaviour. Too many people are mindlessly following the standard advice and a vision of success crafted by a self-interested financial services industry. You have interrogated the conventional wisdom and adopted only what makes sense for you.

Achieving financial freedom is the incremental process of making your life better. It is about worrying less about money, about giving yourself options to pursue the type of life you want, about supporting those you love. We hope this book has helped you focus on what you want out of life and how your finances can help you get there.

Shani's focus going forward

There are a few challenges I foresee in the future.

A large part of my investment strategy is focusing on aspects of performance I can control. This includes taxes and fees. The financial services industry continues to innovate to appeal to retail investors. We've seen this gain momentum particularly in the ETF space as product providers fight for customer share.

I hold some investments where there have been innovations in the investment product industry that provide marginally better alternatives. It's important to consider all costs, though. Selling in and out of investments can significantly reduce investors' return outcomes.

As I mentioned in chapter 12, it's important to be efficient with your investments, but not to the detriment of your total return outcomes. I'll be walking a tightrope between maximising efficiency in my portfolio and maximising my outcomes by reducing costs and taxes.

My challenge moving forward is to resist the temptation to find the 'best' product for me at a set moment in time — when I do my portfolio review. This will become a larger issue for me as my investment balances grow, when even a small fee difference will have an outsized impact on my portfolio.

Another challenge is one faced by any investor who got started in the past 15 years. I've never experienced a proper bear market. I have prepared as much as I can with the right structures around my portfolio to prevent poor behaviour. I can foresee how I will act in this situation, but I have no idea whether this predicts accurately what I will do.

A large part of the unknown is not around me withdrawing funds. It's the fear of missing out on lower valuations and on the ability to capitalise on a downturn. My investment strategy is strictly strategic; I avoid tactical allocations. I want to ensure that my behaviour aligns with what I'm trying to achieve. Lower valuations will mean less risk in my portfolio and the potential for larger gains in the recovery.

I don't want to get into a habit of hoarding cash and deviating from my investment strategy to try to time the market to capture lower valuations. My strategy has worked for me. It will get me to my goals over the long term. I trust that having structures in place and written down, tied to my goals, will give me the best chance of achieving that.

(continued)

I'm also cognisant of the concentration risk in my finances. I work in finance. I invest in Australian markets where the market is concentrated in two industries — including financial services — and a large amount of my wealth is held in my home, with a large mortgage.

We don't know the extent of the next downturn. For peace of mind, I continue to build a buffer in my emergency fund and in my mortgage payments. I want to ensure that the next downturn doesn't set me back irreparably from reaching my financial goals.

It is easier for someone later in their investing life or their career to build a capital base that can protect them for a good amount of time from an event like this, though it's also more difficult for them to get a job. I plan to continue to build on this financial security, as well as contributing to my long-term financial goals.

I don't want to end this book with a list of my worries. These are all manageable, proof that with proper planning you can build the financial security to provide peace of mind and support a better quality of life.

The point of good financial planning is not to have an ironclad plan that can't change. Over your life you will invariably face changes to regulations, taxes, market and economic conditions. You will also change your goals and what you want out of life. Your plan can be adjusted based on changes in circumstances.

I have shared a lot about myself in this book, what I want to achieve and how that has influenced the way I approach my life goals, financial goals and the way I invest. Sharing this much makes me feel vulnerable. Particularly when it's with strangers. But despite this feeling of vulnerability, it has also energised me to know that it may help someone who has gone through similar experiences to realise that investing is for them.

One last story about myself. When I was in high school a careers counsellor handed us a book that reviewed potential careers, the marks we needed to get into university (if a suitable degree was a requirement) and the average salaries. I went through this book and chose the careers with average salaries that I thought would give me a good life. At the time I didn't consider any of the other factors that contribute to a career.

It never occurred to me that I could find a job where I could earn good money as well as enjoy a sense of fulfilment. Luckily I've found that. I get to go to work and help people understand how to live more fulfilling lives and achieve the best financial outcomes they can within their circumstances. I also have the opportunity and resources to build a life that's beyond 'comfortable'. Regardless of the challenges I'll face, I know that over the long term I will have a better and fuller life with less anxiety. How good is that?

Mark's focus going forward

I'm in a decent place financially. I can see the finish line, but that doesn't mean I'm certain of making it. As Nassim Taleb observed, 'It does not matter how frequently something succeeds if failure is too costly to bear.'

It has been a strange journey from extreme saver to living a more balanced life where my financial assets actively help me live the way I want to. I appreciate the position my commitment to saving and investing has put me in, while

(continued)

feeling some regret about missed opportunities to do more when I was younger.

I'm a fairly boring investor and I don't see that changing. I buy boring companies that pay dividends and ETFs that hold boring companies that pay dividends. This allows me to watch the more speculative or exciting parts of the market with a slightly bemused indifference. I just keep chugging along earning returns that generally trail the market in good times and exceed the market in bad times. I've made peace with that, and while I'm not pursuing a pathway to maximise my wealth, I have built resilience into my financial life that should help me weather whatever storms the future holds.

I've seen how life can take paths we don't anticipate. I watched my parents go through divorce in their sixties. Strangely, more than any other it was that event that inspired me to write this book. As in many marriages of that time — and frankly, now — my dad controlled the finances. After the divorce my mother was faced with the task of managing her finances for the first time. Trying to navigate the transition to retirement can challenge the most experienced investor. Having previously relied on my father to deal with all of the family finances, it was a bridge too far for even my Ivy league–educated mother who successfully ran a company.

My mother's problem was not a lack of ability but a lack of confidence and knowledge. I hope this book provides many readers with the knowledge and confidence to take control of their financial futures. And I hope that Shani and I and the team at Morningstar can continue to help spread the message that anyone can improve their investing outcomes. It will take only a little effort to make your life and the lives of the people you care about better.

Where to go from here

'What now?' you may be asking. We believe that everyone can achieve financial freedom, and we are both passionate about making investing information accessible to all Australians. Visit us at Morningstar.com.au. Our content is free, as are our *Investing Compass* podcast, webinars, videos and articles. You'll also find a list of sources and other materials relating to this book. We are here to support you as you continue on your investing journey.

Index

J

K

L

Printed and bound by CPI Group (UK) Ltd, Croydon, CR0 4YY

10/09/2025

14733049-0001